BUBBLE
OR
REVOLUTION?

BUBBLE

OR

REVOLUTION?

*The Present and Future of Blockchain
and Cryptocurrencies*

Neel Mehta
Aditya Agashe
Parth Detroja

To my friends and family, for supporting me no matter how crazy my dreams get —Neel

To my family and friends, thanks for supporting my passion for business and helping me push past my fears to embrace entrepreneurship —Adi

To my friends and family for their never-ending support in my seemingly ridiculous endeavors —Parth

Contents

Introduction

Bitcoin is a tool for freeing humanity from oligarchs and tyrants, dressed up as a get-rich-quick scheme.

— Naval Ravikant, founder of AngelList[1]

Bitcoin is probably rat poison squared.

— Warren Buffett, CEO of Berkshire Hathaway[2]

T HE YEAR was 2017, and the United Nations had a problem. Because of Syria's bloody civil war, ten thousand Syrian refugees had fled to a refugee camp in neighboring Jordan.[3] The UN's World Food Program (WFP) had set up supermarkets in the camp where refugees could buy items like olive oil and lentils, and they needed to give refugees some money to buy these items.[4]

The problem was that just giving refugees prepaid credit cards wouldn't work. This approach had cost the WFP millions in the past due to transaction fees and the need to build partnerships with local banks — money that could have gone toward millions of meals.[5] Giving refugees ID cards that entitled them to goods wouldn't work, either; when the WFP had tried this in the past, local tribal leaders had snatched up refugees' cards and begun trading them as currency.[6]

So the WFP turned to a fledgling technology called the *blockchain*, most famous for being the technology behind the digital currency Bitcoin. Each refugee's "account" was credited with some money, and when a refugee went to a store, they'd verify their identities with an iris scanner and then redeem these credits for food and supplies — all without opening their wallets.[7] The shops could then sell their collected coupons back to the UN.[8]

This project, called Building Blocks, was a smashing success. It slashed money-transfer fees by 98%,[9] reduced fraud, and radically simplified the aid process for both the WFP and refugees.[10]The UN quickly grew the program to serve 100,000 refugees,[11] with a plan to eventually serve all refugees in Jordan.[12]

The benefits to the UN go beyond aid: the UN announced that it might one day be able to track refugees' identities and life history using the blockchain, thus helping refugees find jobs and loans in new countries if their passports or educational records were destroyed.[13]

People around the globe have been incredibly excited about the blockchain and its sister technology, *cryptocurrencies* (such as the aforementioned Bitcoin). The *Harvard Business Review* wondered if the blockchain could upend the staid banking industry,[14] the famous venture capitalist Marc Andreessen said the blockchain was "the most important invention since the internet,"[15] and analysts worldwide believe cryptocurrencies will revolutionize money and technology as we know them.[16]

On the other hand, these mysterious new technologies have also earned a sinister reputation. Drug lords use Bitcoin to peddle drugs anonymously online,[17] cryptocurrencies have been accused of contributing to global warming,[18] and hackers demand payment in Bitcoin so law enforcement can't track them.[19] And even the positive hype around these technologies often seems to go too far: an iced tea company, Long Island Iced Tea, added the word "blockchain" to its name[20] and saw its stock price almost quadruple.[21]

So what's true? Are blockchain and cryptocurrencies a hype-fueled bubble, technologies with no legitimate use cases? Or are they revolutionary inventions that will remake governments, businesses, economies, and societies in their image? In other words: bubble or revolution?

The goal

As the above stories show, blockchain and cryptocurrencies — collectively known as *crypto* — are among the most consequential and yet least understood new technologies of our time. Most public conversations about crypto are dominated by enthusiasts saying crypto will tear down banks and governments and pundits saying crypto is nothing but a scam. Not many people pause to break down how exactly these technologies work and what real potential they have.

In *Bubble or Revolution*, we want to change that. Through real-world examples, plain-English explanations, and unbiased analyses, we want to teach you how crypto works, where it's useful, and where it isn't. We'll tell you what we think of the bubble-or-revolution debate, but we'll also give you the tools you'll need to decide for yourself.

What's inside

In *Bubble or Revolution*, you'll learn about the building blocks of blockchains and cryptocurrencies; explore their strengths and weaknesses using case studies; dive deep into their social, political, economic, and technical implications; and gain insight into their futures from our exclusive interviews with dozens of tech industry leaders.

Just a handful of the things we'll cover:

- The economics of Bitcoin mining
- Famous cryptocurrency hacks and flaws
- Xbox's blockchain for video games
- The SEC's regulation of crypto startups
- Currency tokenization and the future of money

Our first book

When the three of us wrote the business bestseller *Swipe to Unlock: The Primer on Technology and Business Strategy*, we aimed to teach readers everything they'd need to know about the tech world, from the guts of Google's search algorithm to Facebook's high-level business strategies.

Each section in *Swipe to Unlock* is a real-world case study, posing a question you might have had yourself—how Spotify recommends songs, how self-driving cars work, and why Amazon offers free shipping even though it loses them money. We covered a wide range of technologies, from security to cloud computing to machine learning.

But since we wrote *Swipe to Unlock*, cryptocurrencies and blockchains have exploded into the public consciousness in a way that few other technologies have. It's essential that technologists, entrepreneurs, business leaders, and even casual observers understand these technologies — so we decided to write a book about them.

This book will be a deep dive into one key pillar of technology; if you'd like to gain a broader understanding of the tech landscape, frameworks for understanding tech business strategy, and a mental toolkit for evaluating new technologies, you might want to give *Swipe to Unlock* a read as well. Check it out at swipetounlock.com or find it on Amazon.

Who we are

Before we jump in, here's a bit more about us.

Neel Mehta is a product manager at Google and formerly worked at Microsoft and the U.S. government, where he created the federal government's first technology internship program.

Adi Agashe is a product manager at Microsoft and formerly the founder and CEO of Belle Applications.

Parth Detroja is a product manager at Facebook and formerly worked in product and marketing roles at Microsoft, Amazon, and IBM.

Thank you

Thank you again for choosing to read *Bubble or Revolution*! We hope you find this book informative, interesting, and maybe even fun. From all of us — enjoy!

Neel Mehta
namehta.com
linkedin.com/in/neel-a-mehta

Aditya Agashe
adityaagashe.com
linkedin.com/in/adityaagashe
quora.com/profile/Adi-Agashe

Parth Detroja
parthdetroja.com
linkedin.com/in/parthdetroja

Chapter 1.
Bitcoin & the Blockchain

Bitcoin gives us, for the first time, a way for one Internet user to transfer a unique piece of digital property to another Internet user, such that the transfer is guaranteed to be safe and secure, everyone knows that the transfer has taken place, and nobody can challenge the legitimacy of the transfer. The consequences of this breakthrough are hard to overstate.

> —Marc Andreessen, co-founder of Andreessen Horowitz[1]

Trusted third parties are security holes. Anybody in the blockchain space, I would like to get that in their head. That's basically the key to the whole design.

> —Nick Szabo, creator of Bit Gold (a precursor to Bitcoin)[2]

O N HALLOWEEN 2008,[3] a computer scientist who called himself Satoshi Nakamoto published a whitepaper introducing Bitcoin, a digital currency that lets people exchange money without going through a bank, credit card processor, or other financial institution.[4] Nobody knew who Satoshi really was, but everyone on the mailing list where he announced the paper took notice.

With a single email, Satoshi introduced the world to blockchains and cryptocurrencies, a pair of technologies that have become household names. But to understand those technologies, we have to start by unraveling the mysterious scientist's invention.

The trouble with money

Throughout most of human history, there have been two ways to hold money: owning physical items (cash, gold pieces, cattle, salt, etc.) or having a trusted institution like a bank or chieftain track how much money you have.

Both these forms of money have their problems.

The shortcomings of physical, or tangible, forms of money like cash or cows are pretty clear: it's easy to steal, it can't be used for online or long-distance transactions (try buying something with cash from someone in a foreign country), it can often be counterfeited, and it's a pain to store and transport.

Middleman-mediated money

To solve these problems, humanity invented money mediated by a trusted institution like a bank or local chief. Many forms of money and payment fall under this umbrella: bank accounts, bank loans, credit cards, checks, and many of the other financial tools we use these days. By trusting a central institution, or *middleman*, you can solve most of the problems of tangible money:

- You can trust a bank to keep your money safer than you could keep it at home (compare a bank account to stuffing cash under your mattress).
- You can make speedy online and digital payments, since paying someone is as easy as having your bank and their bank update your account balances (which are just numbers on a database somewhere).
- It's harder to make fake money when a trusted authority tracks exactly how much money everyone has. (Since there's no central record of how much cash everyone has, the only way to spot a counterfeiter is to hope you can distinguish fake cash from real cash.)
- If you trust a middleman to hold your money, you don't need to lug any around with you.

This kind of middleman-mediated money really is remarkable. But there's a reason people still use cash and some stores are cash-only: middleman-mediated money (which we'll abbreviate *M3*) has its share of shortcomings, most of which stem from the very fact that there's a middleman.

The first problem: when your money flows through middlemen, you have to play by their rules, which often means having to pay fees. When you pay for something with a credit card, the merchant doesn't get all the money; they have to pay fees to the credit card processor (about 1.5-2.5% for Visa, Mastercard, and Discover, and 2.5-3.5% for American Express).[5][a]

---

[a] The higher fees are one reason why many shops don't take American Express.

Sending money internationally with PayPal will cost you about 3% in fees, and if you're a merchant, accepting payment with PayPal will also cost you about 3%.[6] And the fees for sending money abroad with Western Union, MoneyGram, Xoom, or other remittance companies can be several percent as well.[7]

You can see now why many stores are cash-only or have minimum purchases for you to use credit cards.

Another problem with M3 is that you can only use it if the middlemen grant you access. Practically, this means that the world's two billion unbanked people[8] can't use any money that involves a bank account (which is to say, most of M3), and people with bad or no credit can't use credit cards.

The last big problem with M3 is that you're entrusting them with your money — and, nowadays, your data. Banks are pretty good about not losing your money, but financial institutions' track record with data security is nowhere near as good. Hackers stole data on 100 million JPMorgan customers in 2014,[9] and sensitive information (dates of birth, addresses, etc.) on 100 million Capital One customers was stolen in 2019.[10] That's not to mention perhaps the most infamous hack of all: when the personal data (including Social Security Numbers) of almost 150 million Americans was stolen from Equifax.[11]

In short, tangible money is insecure, inconvenient, easy to fake, and impractical for digital payments. Middleman-mediated money, or M3, solves these problems, but introduces problems of fees, lack of accessibility, and a different form of insecurity. Right now, we have to pick our poison.

Intangibility

But if you think about it, you'll realize that what we really need in money is intangibility. M3 gives you intangibility by introducing middlemen: if you trust institutions to manage and move your money for you, you don't have to hold tangible money anymore. But, of course, middlemen come with their own bundle of drawbacks. Is there a way to cut out the middleman while retaining intangibility? In other words, can you have a form of money that's both intangible *and* middleman-free?

You can probably see what we're getting at here. But it turns out that people invented an intangible, middleman-free form of money centuries before Satoshi introduced Bitcoin to the world. To meet these people, we have to visit the tiny Micronesian island of Yap in the middle of the Pacific Ocean.

Rai stones

The traditional currency on Yap is giant stone rings known as rai stones. These stones are massive: some reach ten feet across[12] and weigh as much as a pickup truck.[13] Each Yap village has dozens of rai stones scattered around town.[14]

A rai stone, a traditional form of money on the Pacific island of Yap. Source: Wikimedia[15]

As you can imagine, people can't lug these stones around the island to pay with them. Instead, the Yapese collectively remember who owns each stone and keep a mental log of past transactions. For instance, if the chieftain's daughter wants to buy a boat from the carpenter, she might announce to the villagers that one rai stone she controls (say, the one on the beach) now belongs to the carpenter. The villagers would spread the word that the chieftain's daughter gave a stone to the carpenter.

Then, if the carpenter wants to give that stone to someone else, the villagers will let him, since everyone's mental records say that that stone now belongs to him.[16] (Roughly speaking, someone can spend a stone if most villagers agree that they own it.)

Intangible

The impressive part of the rai stone system is that all kinds of economic activity can happen without stones physically moving at all; indeed, you can own a stone even if it's clear on the other side of town from your house. In fact, you can even use rai stones if they can never be seen again. Hundreds of years ago, a ship carrying a rai stone sank off the coast. The local villagers reasoned that the stone must still exist somewhere on the ocean floor, so people kept paying each other with the stone as if nothing had happened![17]

In other words, in the rai stone system, the physical location and movement of the stones doesn't matter at all. This stands in stark contrast to traditional tangible money systems, where the physical location and movement of money *does* matter: the only money you own is money in your house or on your person, and the only way you can pay someone is by handing over physical items to them.

This means that the rai stone system is a form of intangible money. It's quite like money in a bank, which we know to be intangible: it doesn't matter where the dollar bills are — or if they even exist at all! — and when you send someone money, no physical items move.

Middleman-free

What's more, the rai stone system is democratic: you own a stone if a majority of your fellow villagers agree that you do. Instead of trusting a single person or institution to track how much money you have, as you would in M3, you diffuse your trust across the whole village.

This democratic system of deciding who owns stones — in other words, *consensus* — has a lot of advantages over a middleman-moderated system. Imagine an alternate universe where the village chieftain kept the official log of payments and stone ownership, instead of the villagers collectively keeping a log via consensus. (In this universe, the Yapese money system would behave a lot like M3; the chieftain would fill the role of a bank.) The chieftain could easily force everyone to pay him a fee to make a payment, steal stones by strategically erasing payments from his logbook, lose his logbook (and thus make the local economy grind to a halt), and so on.

The rai stone system is thus both intangible *and* middleman-free. You get the convenience of M3 — no need to lug stones around town — without the problems of relying on a middleman. It provides an example of that "best of both worlds" money system we talked about in the previous section.

The lesson here is that intangible money systems always require trust: you'll only relinquish physical control over your money if you can trust that something or someone will keep an accurate record of your money. Yap's innovation was realizing that you can place your trust in *systems*, not middlemen; in this case, the trustworthy system was the mental log of transactions that the Yapese villagers all shared. By placing your trust in a shared, consensus-driven system — a group of people who follow shared rules — instead of a single person or entity, you get intangible money without the middleman.

Bitcoin's blockchain

We don't know if Satoshi studied Yap while developing Bitcoin, but his insight was very similar.

Bitcoin is a digital currency, so it's intangible, and it's (in theory) middleman-free because it doesn't rely on a bank or other institution to keep track of people's money balances. Instead, Bitcoin relies on a network of computers around the world to keep a shared log, or *ledger*, of every past payment. This "shared public ledger," as it's known, is called a blockchain, and it's basically a high-tech version of Yapese villagers' shared memory of past payments.

In short, Bitcoin is a modern, internet-friendly version of rai stones. It's both intangible and (in theory) middleman-free, which makes it a compelling alternative to our traditional money systems, which force you to have either tangibility or middlemen.

The shared Google sheet

Another, and more technical, way to think about the blockchain is as a giant Google spreadsheet shared with everyone in the world, with one row per transaction:

	A	B	C	D
1	**Transaction ID**	**From**	**To**	**Amount**
2	1	(origin)	A	50
3	2	(origin)	B	50
4	3	A	C	20
5	4	B	D	25
6	5	D	C	15
7	6	B	A	5

A simplified way to think of the Bitcoin blockchain: it's a Google sheet shared with the whole world.

15

(Naturally, you'd want to make this sheet add-only: you wouldn't want rogue users changing past transactions.)

Anyway, imagine every Bitcoin user in the world has a copy of this spreadsheet stored on their computers. Each time someone makes a new transaction, the transaction is broadcast to everyone, and everyone's computers download new versions of the spreadsheet.

Mining

The one obvious flaw with making such a Google spreadsheet to track payments is that someone could try to spend money they don't have. Clearly, you need somebody to verify transactions before they're submitted so that these problematic transactions don't get through.

In the M3 world, you'd trust a bank or financial institution to do that verification; your bank won't let you transfer money to a friend if you don't have enough money in your account. But in the world of Bitcoin, you can't rely on some trusted person to do the verification; that would defeat the whole purpose of not having middlemen.

Instead, Bitcoin farms out this verification work to members of the community. Any Bitcoin user can use their computer to verify pending transactions and add only the valid transactions to the blockchain. For efficiency's sake, transactions are batched into *blocks* of a few thousand transactions per block.[18]

Incentives

But, of course, people won't do the computational work of verifying transactions for free, so the Bitcoin software has to throw in some money to incentivize them. If you verify a block of transactions, you'll earn some fees from every transaction in the block, and the Bitcoin software will also pay you a fixed chunk of bitcoins,[b] known as the *block reward*. The bitcoins in the block reward don't exist before the verification — the Bitcoin software creates them out of thin air.[19]

Because Bitcoin thinks of itself as a digital version of gold[20] and verifiers put in work to extract brand-new money, this verification process is called *mining*, and the verifiers are known as *miners*. (You're mining with a computer instead of a pick and shovel, but the business model is roughly the same.)

So, if we wanted to return to our Google sheet and make it look more like a real blockchain, we'd add columns for blocks, fees, and rewards, like so:

	A	B	C	D	E	F	G	H
1	Block ID	Transaction ID	From	To	Amount	Miner	Mining Fee	Block Reward
2	B1	T1	A	B	10	C	1	25
3		T2	A	D	15		1	
4		T3	A	E	5		1	
5	B2	T4	B	C	2	E	1	25
6		T5	D	E	5		1	
7		T6	C	A	10		1	

A more advanced model of Bitcoin's blockchain, incorporating mining, fees, and rewards.

So person C mined block B1, which contained three transactions, and earned 28 bitcoins for their trouble: 25 from the block reward and 1 each from each transaction.

---

[b] The currency is called "Bitcoin" with a capital "B," while the units of currency are called "bitcoins," with a lowercase "b." It's like the difference between "the US dollar" (the name of the currency) and "dollars" (the units of currency).

Pop quiz: assuming each person (A, B, C, D, and E) started out with 100 bitcoins, how many do they have after they make these transactions?

The answers:

- Person A sent 10 bitcoins to B and paid a fee of 1 bitcoin, then sent 15 bitcoins to D and paid a fee of 1 bitcoin, then sent 5 bitcoins to E and paid a fee of 1 bitcoin, then received 10 bitcoins. That means A ends up with 100 - 10 - 1 - 15 - 1 - 5 - 1 + 10 = 77 bitcoins.
- Person B earned 10 bitcoins from A and sent 2 bitcoins (plus a 1-bitcoin fee) to C. So B now has 100 + 10 - 2 - 1 = 107 bitcoins.
- Person C earned 25 + 1 + 1 + 1 = 28 bitcoins from mining block B1, so they have 100 + 28 + 2 - 10 - 1 = 119 bitcoins.
- Person D now has 100 + 15 - 5 - 1 = 109 bitcoins.
- Person E also earned 28 bitcoins from mining block B2, so they have 100 + 5 + 28 + 5 = 138 bitcoins.[c]

Blocks and chains

It turns out that our spreadsheet model is just that: a model. It's a simplification. The real Bitcoin blockchain doesn't store blocks in a spreadsheet-like format.

Instead, Bitcoin's blockchain stores blocks in a linear "chain," where each block mathematically points to the last one:[21]

---

[c] Quite a profitable day. We'd all like to be Person E.

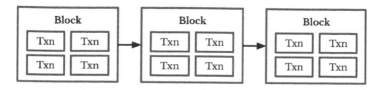

The blockchain stores blocks in a linear chain; "txn" is Bitcoin shorthand for "transaction." Each block refers to the previous one, but computer scientists usually drawn chains like this with the arrows pointing from one block to the next one so it's more intuitive.

This way, the ordering of blocks is clear even though blocks don't explicitly have numbers. Imagine if you took a paperback novel and tore out all the pages, removing all page and chapter numbers as well. Then imagine you scattered the pages all over the floor.

You could still put the pages back in order, though, since each page implicitly references what happened on the last page. (For instance, if page X ends with a character driving up to the courthouse and page Y starts with the character walking into the courthouse, you can be pretty sure page Y comes right after page X.)

Hashing

Bitcoin has no notion of plot, of course, so blocks reference each other with math. Specifically, they use a mathematical technique called *hashing*, where you feed a bunch of information (words, numbers, Bitcoin blocks, etc.) into an algorithm that spits out a short "fingerprint" of the information.[22]

We humans use hashing all the time, such as with initials. A long name can easily be condensed to a few letters: a long name like "John Fitzgerald Kennedy" becomes something short like "JFK."

You have an input (the full name); the *hash function* (the process of taking someone's initials); and an output, or *hash* (the initials).

Computers use fancier hash functions — the most popular ones are the MD5[23] or SHA-256[24] algorithms — but the core idea is the same: large inputs of data become short outputs.

In Bitcoin, each block has an associated hash. Each block's hash is based partly on the hash of the block before it.[d] This way, each block refers to the block before it. So, if you got an unordered list of blocks and their associated hashes, you could pretty easily put the blocks back in order, just like the person who could arrange pages by looking at the plot connections.

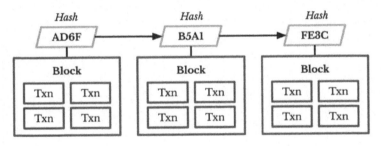

Blocks are chained together using their hashes; each hash is computed from (among other things) the hash of the previous block.

(What's up with the numbers and letters in the hashes? Hashes are written in the *hexadecimal,* or *base-16,* format.[e] They're also much longer than 4 characters,[25] but our shortened versions are good enough for now.)

---

[d] We'll explain exactly how the hash works in just a few pages.
[e] See Appendix A to learn about hexadecimal and other number systems.

So, Bitcoin batches transactions in blocks, and links them to each other in a chain. Block, meet chain.

Branches and fraud

Look back at our hash-based chaining system and you'll notice that it doesn't actually require blocks to be put into a linear chain. Nothing's stopping you from having two or more blocks come right after a given block:

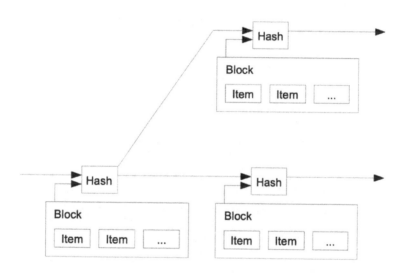

Multiple blocks can cite any given block as their predecessor, so the blockchain can (and does) branch. Image adapted from: Satoshi Nakamoto[26]

The blocktree

As a result, the blockchain doesn't have to be a linear chain. In fact, it usually isn't. The blockchain tends to look more like a "blocktree," with a "trunk" and "branches":

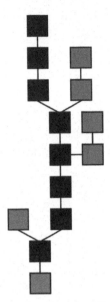

The blockchain can have many branches, just like a tree (imagine the bottom block is at ground level and this diagram looks a lot like a tree.) The longest branch is considered the "official" one. Source: Wikipedia[27]

The blocktree sometimes grows a new branch when two miners generate (or "mine") a block at the same time. This is rare, but it does happen. When it does, there are two transactions splitting off the most recent transaction, and a new branch of the blocktree is born.[28]

But, as with the rai stone system, Bitcoin needs to have a single, linear history of transactions. You can't allow multiple branches to coexist. (Can you imagine telling someone, "in one version of history, I have $500, but in the other version, I have $600"?)

The longest-chain rule

To have a linear official history, Bitcoin uses a rule of thumb called the *longest chain rule*, which says that the branch of the "blocktree" with the most blocks in it is the official blockchain.[29] The longest chain determines how much money you really have, what past transactions have happened, and so on. If it's not on the longest chain, it effectively didn't happen.

The Bitcoin software, which runs on Bitcoin users' computers, enforces the longest chain rule by only paying miners who added a block to the longest chain.[30] This is usually enough to keep miners in line. (It has an unfortunate side effect, though. If two miners mine a block at the same time, two branches are born, and only one branch is going to win out and become the longest chain. The other branch becomes "orphaned" and is thrown out, and the unlucky miner who mined the block at the base of that branch gets no money. These "orphanings" happen a few times a day.[31])

Chain hijacking

But the longest chain rule still leaves a security hole. What if a crooked miner created a new branch and mined blocks faster than everyone else, thus making her branch longer than the legitimate branch? Well, the crooked miner's branch would become the longest chain, so it would become the official blockchain. All the blocks on her fraudulent chain would become official history, and some of the blocks on the legitimate chain would get thrown out.

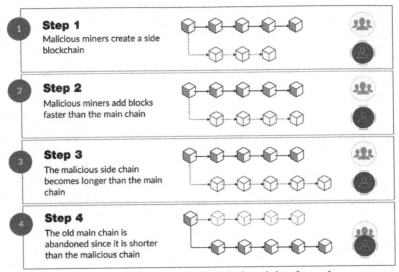

Step 1
Malicious miners create a side blockchain

Step 2
Malicious miners add blocks faster than the main chain

Step 3
The malicious side chain becomes longer than the main chain

Step 4
The old main chain is abandoned since it is shorter than the malicious chain

How an attacker could hijack the blockchain by mining faster than everyone else.

Letting a scammer control the blockchain would cause a lot of chaos, of course, but it could also lead to fraud. Imagine the crooked miner buys thousands of dollars of merchandise with Bitcoin and puts that transaction on the blockchain. She then executes her attack, building a new chain longer than the official chain. The transaction where she paid the merchant gets thrown out since it's no longer on the longest chain; it's as if she'd never made the payment in the first place. So now, she's gotten all her merchandise, but she never had to pay for it!

Game of nonces

How do you stop attacks like these? You have to make it hard for attackers to mine faster than the honest miners. To do that, Satoshi made it very time-consuming to mine a block.

The process Satoshi designed begins with the transactions. Transactions waiting to be vetted and confirmed sit around in the *transaction pool*, also known as the *memory pool* or *mempool*[32]. When you want to mine a block, you choose a few thousand transactions from the pool, verify them, and build your block.

Then all you have to do is generate a hash for your block, and you'll be able to put it on the chain and get your rewards.

But generating the hash isn't easy. It requires three inputs: the last block's hash, the transactions, and a special number that you pick called a *nonce*.

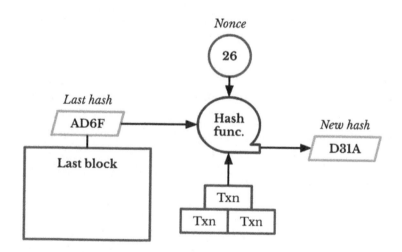

The hash function uses three inputs to generate the hash for a block.

The catch is that the hash value is different for each nonce, and you're only allowed to add your block to the chain if your hash starts with the right number of zeroes. So if the nonce you picked doesn't lead to a good hash, you have to try again and again:

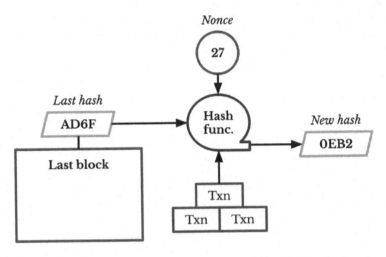

Changing the nonce gives you a completely different output hash.

Guess and check

What makes this hard is that there's no discernible pattern in the hashes; you can't predict the hash from the input, and even small changes to the input make the output entirely different. If you run the word "cat" through the popular MD5 hash function, you get this inscrutable output:

d077f244def8a70e5ea758bd8352fcd8.

Meanwhile, the MD5 hash of "bat" is not even close:

5f3f4681121b460e3304a1887f42f1c3.

What's more, hash functions used by computers tend to be so-called *one-way functions*: it's easy to compute the output given the input, but it's nearly impossible to guess the input given the output.

Human initials are kind of like this: if you see the initials GMD, it's not immediately obvious what the original name was.[f]

This means that the only way to "crack" a hash function — to figure out the input given the output — would be to guess every single output. Brute-forcing computers' hash functions is incredibly difficult: cracking the SHA-256 hash function, which Bitcoin uses for hashing, would take millions of years[33] and cost, in all likelihood, millions or billions of dollars.[34][g]

In other words, you can't try to reverse-engineer a good nonce. So the only way to mine a block is to guess nonces over and over until you win — like playing a digital lottery. We call it the game of nonces. (The word *nonce* comes from "number used only once," since you try it once and throw it out if it's no good.[35])

Try your hand

It's instructive to simulate this game. Go to <u>md5online.org</u>, a site that (as the name implies) lets you run text through the MD5 hash function.[36] Your challenge is to pick a nonce that, when put after the word "hello," yields a hash that starts with a zero.

You might start by choosing a nonce of 1, so your hash input would be "hello1." The MD5 hash of that text is

203ad5ffa1d7c650ad681fdff3965cd2.

---

[f] If you're wondering, we were thinking of George Mifflin Dallas, the obscure 11th Vice President of the United States, serving from 1845 to 1849.

[g] The exact difficulty depends on how complex your input text is. If your password is "hello" and you hash it with SHA-256, it's pretty easy to break, since it's likely that someone on the internet has posted the SHA-256 hash of "hello." A simple Google search of the hash would reveal the input.

No dice. You might then choose a nonce of 2; the MD5 hash of "hello2" is

6e809cbda0732ac4845916a59016f954.

That's no good either.

If you keep increasing the nonce by one, you'll eventually find that the first nonce that yields a winning hash is 33: the MD5 hash of "hello33" is

005529451481309d2b8f708bbb81ea41.

Success!

This wasn't that hard, and mathematically speaking, it shouldn't be. MD5 hashes are written in the hexadecimal, or base-16, number system, meaning that each digit is one of 16 possible characters (0-9 and A-F) .[h] Hashes are pretty much random, so the first digit of any hash has a 1/16 chance of being a zero. That means you'll get a successful hash once out of every 16 tries, on average. Counting up from 1 happened to be unlucky, since it took us 33 tries.

Nonce	Input	MD5 Hash
29	hello29	fc12c051dd3eb4d7beb430f362522fda
30	hello30	868594340dd4f911fcbdbebf80dbdcaa
31	hello31	5cebee1d96882e6325b758a1fbd80b02
32	hello32	ce62f2f1d58fe37381a2ac08fc544467
33	hello33	005529451481309d2b8f708bbb81ea41

---

[h] See Appendix A to learn more about number systems like base-16.

34	hello34	45c66648b3d94b4e46a6ba796fbee7af
35	hello35	44ee8f3e8ef0f8e7085193d123b20a9e
36	hello36	092962df00b7139faca15313ff345c4e
37	hello37	c1b4349f3222aec9916dd1fbe65c02fe
38	hello38	ebcd88fab0212bad35bde21c11185754
39	hello39	2206e08b5186fc0c5d4239259f09037f
40	hello40	5886c943b32a6dd596b19b5897c0306d
41	hello41	20ce5b4e49c7847661a9bf6edfd35760

The hash output is effectively random, so you have to keep guessing nonces until you get a lucky hash. The first winning nonce in this case is 33.

Now imagine if you had to pick a nonce that yielded a hash with at least *four* leading zeroes. Then, only one out of every 16^4 = 65,536 nonces would yield a winning hash. (If you're curious, the smallest winning nonce is 105,484; the MD5 hash of "hello105484" is

$$0000049898d233686087e44bc2a1c97a$$

which actually has five leading zeroes. Don't worry, we wrote code to guess this.[37])

Trying to guess the right nonce for Bitcoin mining is even harder. At the time of writing, each nonce you try gives you a 1 in roughly 66,000,000,000,000,000,000,000 (that's 66 with 21 zeroes, or 66 billion trillion) chance of mining a block.[38][39] That huge number isn't far off from the number of stars in the universe.[40]

Arm yourself

It's hard to overstate just how hard it is to guess a good nonce and, by extension, mine a block. If you tried using a MacBook to run the mining algorithm, it would take you about two million years to guess a successful nonce.[41][i]

For obvious reasons, serious miners don't use their laptops to mine. Instead, they buy powerful computers outfitted with hyper-specialized computer chips called *ASICs*, or *Application-Specific Integrated Circuits*,[42]. ASICs are specially wired to run Bitcoin's hashing algorithm very, very quickly,[j] meaning that they can guess nonces with blazing speed, but they can't do anything else.[43]

An ASIC that specializes in running Bitcoin's hashing algorithm. Source:
Wikimedia[44]

---

[i] Assuming Bitcoin's difficulty score is 15.5 trillion, as it is at the time of writing, and that a MacBook can compute one billion hashes per second (1 GH/s).
[j] There are other kinds of ASICs, such as ASICs that specialize in machine learning or image processing, but in the context of cryptocurrencies the term always refers to chips that specialize in mining.

These powerful computers, along with their ASICs, are very powerful but come at a steep cost. One mid-tier, ASIC-equipped mining computer that sells for $2000 can compute about 56 trillion hashes per second (TH/s), meaning it can try 56 trillion nonces a second.[45] But since it's so hard to guess the right nonce, even hardware this powerful would take about 38 years to mine a block, at the time of writing.[46k]

The AntMiner S17 Pro, a $2000 computer that can churn out 56 trillion hashes per second. Source: MiningCrate[47]

In other words, mining bitcoins boils down to a game of mindlessly rolling a multi-trillion-sided die for decades, hoping you get a lucky roll.

---

[k] Assuming Bitcoin's difficulty score is 15.5 trillion (as it is at the time of writing).

Proof of work

If this system seems wasteful, that's because it is, and it was designed that way to make life harder for attackers.

Since the hardest part of mining is guessing the right nonce, and guessing the right nonce depends on how many nonces you try, people with more powerful computers have higher chances of getting the lucky nonce that lets them mine a block. The stronger your computer, the faster you can mine blocks.

Another way to look at it: your mining speed is proportional to the fraction of the world's total *hash power* (the sum of every miner's hashes per second) that you control.

Think back to our example of the crooked miner who wanted to mine a fraudulent chain that was longer than the legitimate chain. To pull this off, she'd need to be able to mine blocks faster than all the other "honest" miners put together, so she'd need to control just over 50% of the world's hash power. This attack, known as a *51% attack*,[48] is possible, but it would probably be prohibitively expensive for our aspiring thief to buy all those ASIC-powered supercomputers. And, unless this attacker could control 51% of the hash power, she would stand no chance of tampering with the blockchain.

In short, to mine bitcoins, you have to put in a lot of work (and a lot of money, since these ASICs don't come cheap.) For this reason, the Bitcoin mining system is known as *proof-of-work*: the winners are those who can work the most for it.[49] If mining was easy as running a few lines of code, attackers could easily hijack the blockchain; making mining hard with the game of nonces is Bitcoin's way of deterring attackers.

Credentials

There's one last piece to this Bitcoin and blockchain puzzle. How do you make sure nobody falsely sends transactions in your name? In the M3 world, you can only send money (like a Venmo transaction or a bank transfer) if you log into your account. Your account details, like your username and password, are held by a trusted financial institution like Venmo or your bank.

But, of course, the whole point of Bitcoin is to avoid middlemen. So usernames and passwords, which require you to trust someone to keep them, won't work. Indeed, there shouldn't be a central place to "sign up" at all. Then how do you let users manage their money?

Decentralized accounts

Bitcoin does this by relying on math and probability. The primary way to have middleman-free, or *decentralized*, sign-up is to let people choose their own usernames and passwords. But without a central server, users can't check if their desired usernames are taken. The solution: make users choose one of trillions of random "usernames," offering such a huge set of potential names that there's a vanishingly small chance of anyone getting a name that's already taken.

The next complication is having a system for checking passwords without a central server. Bitcoin solves this by using one-way functions (like the hash functions we met earlier) to compute the user's "username" from their "password": to prove that they own a "username," users have to provide the "password" that turns into the "username" when run through those functions. (Remember, it should be impossible to guess the "password" from the "username.")

We put the words "username" and "password" in quotes because Bitcoin doesn't use those terms.

For Bitcoin, it starts with your *private key*, a long, totally-random number that only you should know. It's usually written as a 52-character alphanumeric string; this encoding scheme is known as base-58.[50][1] The private key fills the role of a password in Bitcoin.

From the private key, you can run a one-way function called the Elliptic Curve Digital Signature Algorithm, or ECDSA,[51] to generate an intermediary number called the *public key*.

Then you apply two more one-way functions (**SHA-256** of Bitcoin mining fame[52] and another one called **RIPEMD-160**[53]) and do a few more mathematical tweaks to get a more compressed version of the public key,[54] called the *address*.[55] The address is usually written as 26-35 alphanumeric characters,[56] again encoded with base-58. The address is the closest thing Bitcoin has to a username: it's public and is used to identify you.

You can randomly generate your very own Bitcoin private key and address at <u>generatepaperwallet.com</u>.[57] (People usually omit the public key since it's an intermediary.) Using the tool, we generated a private key of

L3QwdtohEnUvkUDXH6KDyN1RLF2uLYNQ1qeyp8mmL6cNvZskorD W

and an address of

12zQuwSVdSo7YhU6sjLnYuni2K24jZR8AA.

---

[1] See Appendix A to learn about base-58 and other number systems.

We could now use those credentials to receive and send money. (Of course, so could you, and so could anyone else reading this book.) Note that the private key and address are just made by algorithms, so you could make them without even connecting to the internet; you don't need to "register" them with anyone.

We generated a random private key and address here. Don't send money to the address, since anyone with the private key can access the money. This image is called a paper wallet; *it lets you print out your private key so you can save it in a secure place.*[58]

Transaction signing

Once you have a private key and address, you can start sending and receiving bitcoins. To prove that you're the sender of a transaction, you digitally "sign" it by using your private key to make a "tag" on the transaction. Anybody can use your public key (which is, of course, visible to everyone) to confirm that you were the one who applied the tag, but nobody can reverse-engineer your private key from the tag.[59]

This system works just like the ink signatures we use on checks, legal documents, and such. Anyone can see your signature, and you can compare a new signature to a known signature to check if the same person made both. And, crucially, you shouldn't be able to forge a signature just by looking at it.

The transparent safe

Bitcoin goes a step farther than conventional username-password schemes, in fact: because all transactions are publicly listed on the blockchain, anyone see the past transactions and Bitcoin balances of any address. We like to think of Bitcoin "accounts" as a transparent safe: anyone can see how much money is inside, but only the person with the private key can use the money.

This is a remarkable property. No other form of money, besides rai stones, offers this kind of transparency.[60] It gives analysts a powerful way to understand the state of the Bitcoin economy, helps track down cybercriminals who use Bitcoin,[61] and makes it easy to prove that you made a payment. But, of course, it means there isn't as much privacy.

Putting the "crypto" in currency

Stepping back, you'll notice that Bitcoin uses a lot of math: hash functions for mining, one-way functions for generating keys and addresses, and digital signatures for proving your identity. These are all forms of *cryptography*, the science of keeping information secure by encoding (or *encrypting*) it in a format that attackers can't reverse-engineer.[62]

For this reason, Bitcoin is called a *cryptocurrency*.[63] Satoshi's insight was that cryptography lets you have a currency that is secure yet transparent — and that's the heart of Bitcoin.

Chapter 2.

Bitcoin Economics

There are 3 eras of currency: Commodity based, politically based, and now, math based.
—Chris Dixon, co-founder of Hutch (acquired by eBay)[1]

To be successful, money must be both a medium of exchange and a reasonably stable store of value. And it remains completely unclear why BitCoin should be a stable store of value.
—Paul Krugman, Nobel laureate in Economics[2]

B ITCOIN has come a long way since Satoshi's announcement: billions of dollars' worth of bitcoins are now exchanged each day,[3] and there are now over $100 billion in coins in circulation.[4] But while this unusual new currency operates with some unusual new rules, we can learn a lot about it by applying our tried-and-true economic lenses.

The $300 million pizzas

As you're surely aware, bitcoins are worth thousands of dollars apiece, and there are countless stories of teenagers becoming millionaires thanks to a lucky (or shrewd) Bitcoin investment.[5] (One choice quote from one of those newly-rich teens: "if you do not become a millionaire in the next ten years" investing in Bitcoin, then "it's your own fault."[6])

But if you think harder about it, it seems pretty strange that digital tokens that an anonymous computer scientist invented out of thin air are worth anything, let alone thousands of dollars each. If you made an app that handed out virtual tokens to all comers, people probably wouldn't line up to start buying them from each other, create forums to discuss tiny swings in the price of your tokens, or build massive companies around your tokens. And yet that's effectively what happened with Satoshi's invention.

Bitcoins didn't become worth thousands each overnight. At the start, they were indeed just toys used by a clever bit of software. But slowly, people started believing that they were valuable enough to throw real money after. That story, like many great stories, started over pizza.

Laszlo's deal

In March 2010, the first *Bitcoin exchange* was launched. This website let you trade bitcoins for dollars and vice versa; the exchange rate at launch was 0.3¢ per bitcoin.[7]

In May of that year, a Florida man named Laszlo Hanyecz posted on a Bitcoin forum offering 10,000 bitcoins (then worth $41, or 0.4¢ each[8]) to anyone who would send him a pizza. He was pretty flexible: "you can make the pizza yourself" or "order it for me from a delivery place," he said. But he insisted on "no weird fish topping or anything like that" (a good call).[9]

The pizzas that Laszlo Hanyecz bought for 10,000 bitcoins in 2010.
Source: Laszlo Hanyecz[10]

A young British man named Jeremy Sturdivant obliged,[11] ordering him two large pizzas from Papa John's.[12] It was the first time anyone had ever bought a real-world item with bitcoins.[13]

The 10,000 bitcoins that Hanyecz paid are now worth over $300 million.[14a]

The price of a single bitcoin has skyrocketed from 0.4¢ each to, at the time of writing, over $30,000 each.[15] That's a 7.5 million-fold increase in about a decade; the price has more than quadrupled every year, on average. No stock, bond, property, or other conventional financial asset can come even close to that rate of growth.

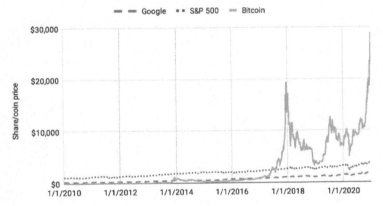

Comparing the growth of Bitcoin, the S&P 500, and Google's stock from 2010 to 2020. Bitcoin is far more volatile than the others, but in exchange it's grown far, far faster. Data source: Google Finance and Blockchain.com[16]

The question is: how did Bitcoin grow that quickly? And how did this digital token that started off as a toy get any monetary value at all?

---

[a] We always cite the price of bitcoins at the time of writing — but since Bitcoin's exchange rate is so volatile, we suggest you look up the most recent rate as you read.

Intersubjective reality

Most of the money we use today has this same philosophical problem as Bitcoin. If you're stranded in the jungle or on Mars, a $20 bill is just a useless piece of paper. But if you're in a store, you can get pizza, socks, can openers, and all manner of other goods in exchange for that piece of paper. In fact, people will even drive you around town, mow your lawn, or watch your dog if you give them that paper. What gives? How does a piece of paper get so much real value?

It boils down to what the historian Yuval Noah Harari calls an *intersubjective reality*[17]: you think this thing has value because you know that *other people* think it has value. A farmer at a farmer's market will gladly give you some homemade jam for a $20 bill because she knows other people will give her groceries, farm supplies, and other items for that $20 bill. And so on.

Bitcoin works the same way: Sturdivant bought pizzas for Hanyecz because he knew he could eventually exchange the 10,000 bitcoins for something else of value (dollars, British pounds, or physical goods). Similarly, people today will buy a bitcoin off you for upwards of $30,000 because they know *other* people will give them goods, services, or cash in exchange for it later (hopefully more than they paid you for the bitcoin).

Wampum belts

These intersubjective realities are fickle things: they fall apart if people stop believing in them. Before Europeans arrived in North America, shell beads known as wampum were used as money up and down the East Coast of what is now the United States. These beads were often strung into elaborate jewelry and belts for easy transportation.[18]

A wampum belt; these belts were used by many Native Americans as a form of money before the American Revolution. Source: Wikimedia[19]

Back then, a Native American chief with enough wampum belts could pay for a giant feast or finance the construction of a giant earthwork (with buildings dedicated to him on top, of course).

How? Because people in the next tribe over would accept the wampum as payment. That tribe would accept wampum as payment because they knew that yet *other* tribes would also take wampum as payment, and so on. Even early European colonists used wampum as a form of money because they knew tribes would accept it.[20]

Wampum had value because of an intersubjective reality. But, by the mid-1700s, that intersubjective reality evaporated as European money took over. It probably started when a few big tribes stopped accepting wampum; then their neighboring tribes probably abandoned it because they could no longer use it to trade with those big tribes; then the tribes around *those* tribes probably abandoned it, and so on.

Because people's acceptance of wampum depended on others' acceptance of wampum, there was a sort of domino effect: a small shock to the wampum system led to the widespread collapse of the wampum currency. Eventually, even Native American tribes demanded to be paid in silver (which, ironically enough, also has value because of intersubjective reality.)[21]

So the story of wampum shows that intersubjective realities can have vicious feedback loops: when a few people quit, everyone quits. But, on the flip side, Bitcoin's rapid rise shows that these feedback loops can be useful too: as a few people (including Hanyecz and Sturdivant) started believing that bitcoins have value, more and more people got on board.[b] Today, the whole world believes bitcoins are worth real money; some people believe in them so much that they even put some of their retirement savings into Bitcoin.[22c]

Bitcoin is flourishing now that people believe it has value; the hardest part was kicking off the positive feedback loop by getting the first people to believe in it. This is why Hanyecz's pizza purchase was so important: it was the first time the world saw that somebody thought bitcoins were economically valuable tools, not just novelties.

Money supply

Intersubjective reality explains why Bitcoin has value in the first place, but the question now is why Bitcoin has achieved its multi-million-fold price jump. This is the million-dollar (or thousand-

---

[b] This isn't all that different from how a social network works: the network gets more useful as more people join, so it can grow exponentially, but it can swiftly collapse for the same reason. These positive feedback loops are also known as *network effects*.
[c] We're not here to make investment advice, but regardless, it's impressive that Bitcoin has become seen as a legitimate investment option.

bitcoin?) problem, but like many economic questions, it comes down to supply and demand.[d]

Economic value comes from scarcity (try selling sand in the desert), and scarcity can come from supplies being limited.[23] So one way that Bitcoin maintains its value is by restricting the *money supply*: the number of bitcoins in circulation is artificially capped, and it's growing more slowly every passing day.[24]

Slowing rewards

Recall that miners' block reward, one of the ways they get paid, includes brand-new bitcoins. This is, in fact, the only way for new bitcoins to get introduced to the world. The Bitcoin software automatically calibrates the *difficulty* of mining (the number of zeroes that have to be at the front of every hash) so that one block is mined, on average, every 10 minutes, so a batch of new coins is created every 10 minutes.

The catch is that the block reward is always decreasing: the Bitcoin software halves the reward every four years. The original block reward was 50 bitcoins per block back in 2008; the reward got halved to 25 bitcoins in 2012; and it got halved again to 12.5 bitcoins in 2016.[25] The most recent halving, at the time of writing, happened in May 2020, when the block reward fell to 6.25 bitcoins per block.[26e]

---

[d] If you want to learn about see macroeconomic theories and equations, see Appendix B.

[e] Note that the price of a bitcoin has grown far faster than the block reward has shrunk, so mining a block still earns you more *dollars* than it did in the past.

Bitcoins mined over time

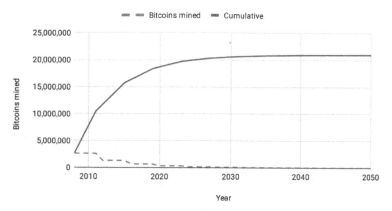

The number of bitcoins mined each year is decaying exponentially, leading the cumulative number of bitcoins mined to plateau. Data source: Bitcoin Wiki[27]

If you extend this trend, you'll find that the block reward will officially hit zero in 2140 after the 33rd halving.[f] At that point, 21 million bitcoins will have been mined, and the supply of bitcoins will never grow again.[28]

But, because of exponential decay, the money supply will have effectively hit that plateau by the mid-2030s, when 99% of all available bitcoins will have been mined. After that point, the supply growth will be cut to a trickle. (In the 40 years from 2100 to 2140, a grand total of 1 bitcoin will be mined.)[29] And we're closer to that plateau than you might think: 85% of all available bitcoins had been mined by summer 2019.[30]

This strategy of ever-slowing supply growth actually makes a lot of sense. Capping the money supply lets Bitcoin ensure the coins are

---

[f] The smallest subdivision of a bitcoin is one-ten-millionth of a bitcoin, known as a *satoshi*. After the halving of 2140, the block reward will round down to zero satoshis.

always scarce and thus valuable. The smooth tapering off of growth helps prevent sudden shocks. Keeping block rewards and thus money supply growth higher in the early days incentivized miners to join early,[31] which helped get the fledgling currency off the ground.[32]

Coin loss

Interestingly, the supply of bitcoins might actually *fall* over time. Bitcoin's highly-decentralized system means that there's no way to recover your bitcoins if you lose your private key; there's no authority like a bank you can ask to reset your "password" for you, and of course, it's nearly impossible to recover your private key given just your public key or address.[33][g] This means that if you store your private key on an external hard drive and spill lemonade on it (which happened to an unlucky Welsh man[34]), rendering it useless, the bitcoins associated with that private key can never again be accessed.

Bitcoins could be lost forever in plenty of other ways. If you get bored and stop using your Bitcoin *wallet* (a piece of software that tracks your private keys and addresses), those coins will sit there for eternity; nobody will ever be able to use them.

Something similar happened to Satoshi: in the first-ever Bitcoin block (called the *genesis block*),[35] Satoshi awarded 50 bitcoins to the address

1A1zP1eP5QGefi2DMPTfTL5SLmv7DivfNa

---

[g] Even the world's most powerful supercomputer would take millions of years to crack the SHA-256 hash algorithm that Bitcoin uses to compute addresses; it would effectively have to guess every single private key.

which he presumably owns. Due to a glitch in the Bitcoin software, those coins can never be moved out of that address.[36] Satoshi has never moved *any* money out of that address,[37] but that hasn't stopped Bitcoin enthusiasts from sending small "offerings" to this address, many with notes of gratitude to Satoshi.[38]

Fee	0.00000146 BTC (0.649 sat/B - 0.255 sat/WU -		+0.00000558 BTC
Hash	3174f91b36d7b18b18dc72a...		2020-01-24 19:13
	bc1qex... 0.00038754 BTC ⊕	➡	1A1zP1... 0.00002000 BTC ⊕
			bc1qex... 0.00036608 BTC ⊕
Fee	0.00000146 BTC (0.649 sat/B - 0.255 sat/WU -		+0.00002000 BTC
Hash	cc795179d5b8246a0f61f81...		2020-01-24 17:06
	bc1qex... 0.00039458 BTC ⊕	➡	1A1zP1... 0.00000558 BTC ⊕
			bc1qex... 0.00038754 BTC ⊕
Fee	0.00000146 BTC (0.649 sat/B - 0.255 sat/WU -		+0.00000558 BTC
Hash	6816bbff7990926d32f69a4...		2020-01-23 17:53
	bc1qex... 0.00040162 BTC ⊕	➡	1A1zP1... 0.00000558 BTC ⊕
			bc1qex... 0.00039458 BTC ⊕
Fee	0.00000146 BTC (0.649 sat/B - 0.255 sat/WU -		+0.00000558 BTC

Several Satoshi well-wishers sent Satoshi's address 0.00000558 bitcoins (BTC), which were worth 50¢ at the time. It's like throwing two quarters in a wishing well for good luck! Source: Blockchain.com[39]

It's actually pretty common for bitcoins to be lost forever: by one estimate, 30% of all mined bitcoins have been lost.[40] If the true rate of bitcoin loss is greater than the rate of block rewards being created, then Bitcoin's supply is actually *shrinking*.

Money demand

Fortunately for us, the supply of bitcoins is easy to quantify and predict; there are formulas that let us calculate exactly how many bitcoins will have been mined at any point in the future.

But unfortunately, it's far harder to make sense of the demand for bitcoins. There's no single number you can point to as a measurement of demand, and it's hard to make mathematical projections about where demand will go in the future.

The buzz theory

The demand story was relatively clear in the early days of Bitcoin (2014 and earlier), when Bitcoin was just taking off. During this time, the primary limiting factor on Bitcoin demand was just that nobody had heard of it, so whenever the news media covered Bitcoin,[41] there was a predictable boost in the demand for, and thus the price of, Bitcoin. In 2014, researchers found that a 1% jump in the number of articles mentioning Bitcoin raised the price of Bitcoin by an average of 0.3%[42] (or, in investor-speak, 30 *basis points* — one basis point is 0.01%[43]).

A lot of the media coverage was negative toward Bitcoin: some of the top stories in those days were the 2014 hack of 740,000 bitcoins from the Bitcoin exchange Mt. Gox (then the largest in the world)[44] and the US government's 2013 takedown of the Silk Road, an online drug marketplace that only accepted Bitcoin.[45] But, as the saying goes, all publicity is good publicity; Bitcoin's price skyrocketed from $13 in January 2013 to over $1100 by that December.

Internet buzz and word-of-mouth were even more powerful factors: those same researchers found that a 1% jump in the number of Google searches for Bitcoin raised the price of Bitcoin by an average of 0.5% (50 basis points).[46]

Indeed, the link between Bitcoin's price and the public interest in the technology (as measured by the total number of Bitcoin trades) was crystal-clear until mid-2014:

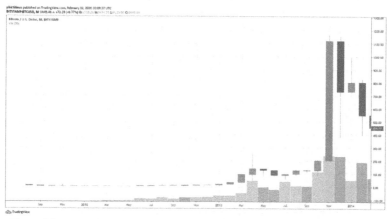

From 2011 to mid-2014, there was a strong correlation between Bitcoin's price (top set of bars) and the volume of Bitcoin trades (bottom set of bars). Source: TradingView[47]

In short, when lack of awareness was the main thing holding Bitcoin back, each additional bit of publicity drove more interest, which drove more trades, which drove Bitcoin's price up.

Unfortunately, that correlation completely collapsed after the mid-2014 spike and crash in Bitcoin's price. From 2014 to 2016, Bitcoin's trading volume was fairly volatile while its price was relatively flat. And from 2017 until the time of writing, the volume has been relatively consistent while the price has jumped around wildly:

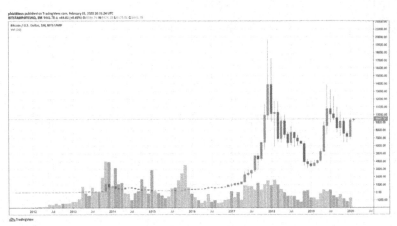

Since mid-2014, there's been little correlation between Bitcoin's price (top bars) and trading volume (bottom bars). Source: TradingView[48]

Why did this happen? Our take is that, after mid-2014, Bitcoin had become a household name (at least among investors), so familiarity was no longer the main driver of demand or price. Thus, analyzing trading volumes and media coverage isn't enough.

The ease-of-use theory

So what are the new factors driving Bitcoin demand? One theory is that Bitcoin is an alternative to the stock market; investors will flock to Bitcoin (raising the demand for bitcoins) when the stock market falters.[49] The problem with this theory, though, is that serious investors don't really see Bitcoin as a strong *hedge* against a stock market tumble. Bitcoin's price is largely uncorrelated with the stock market's performance, so if the stock market falls, Bitcoin will have a roughly 50% chance of falling as well — not a great insurance policy.[50]

We think there are two more realistic factors driving Bitcoin demand. One is that Bitcoin has been getting steadily easier to invest in. In the mid-2010s, the primary way to own bitcoins was to run clunky software on your computer, find a Bitcoin exchange (and hope it was legitimate), and, in some cases, handle irritating cross-border bank payments just to get your hands on some coins.[51] Bitcoin investing was only for the truly dedicated.

But now, anyone can invest in Bitcoin: you can buy bitcoins on sleek websites with a debit card,[52] you can buy and send bitcoins with an app,[53] popular stock-trading apps let you buy bitcoins just like you'd buy stocks,[54] and you can even buy Bitcoin ETFs (*exchange-traded funds*, or baskets of investments) through an ordinary stock broker like Fidelity or TD Ameritrade.[55] Lowering the barrier to entry has removed another cap on Bitcoin demand.

The speculation theory

The other factor, and the more powerful one in our view, is plain old speculation. The majority of Bitcoin users are speculators[56] hoping to make a buck. Bitcoin's highly-volatile price, relative lack of regulation compared to the stock market, and newly-lowered barrier to entry makes it an exciting and relatively easy investment for speculation, especially for younger people.[57]

Despite all of Bitcoin's historic spikes and crashes, Bitcoin's price has generally trended upward over time; analysts think this is because people who buy in are often hesitant to sell even after crashes, holding onto their bitcoins in the hope that the price will eventually rise again.[58] (This is the infamous trend known as *HODLing*.[59]) When people never get rid of their bitcoins, the demand for bitcoins keeps marching ever higher.

In sum, it's hard to measure or predict the demand for bitcoins, but it looks like the demand will keep slowly increasing over time. This, we think, is the main reason why Bitcoin's price — despite all the spikes and crashes — has tended to increase in the long run.

Since the supply for bitcoins will grow more and more slowly with each passing year, the demand will become a bigger and bigger factor in Bitcoin's price. If the upward trend in demand continues, Bitcoin will keep getting more valuable — but if the demand vanishes, Bitcoin's value will collapse.

Combine the consistently low supply and the high yet mercurial demand and you get Bitcoin's price history: wildly volatile yet increasing over the long run. Will these trends continue? Supply will definitely stay restricted, but it's hard to predict demand.

Inflation-proof?

Bitcoin fans like to assert that Bitcoin is immune to inflation because the money supply is capped and is controlled by an algorithm, not people. The argument is that national governments, when given total leeway to print money and adjust interest rates (two big ways central banks can adjust the money supply of "normal" currencies like dollars and pesos), can create massive, crippling inflation, either out of malice or sheer incompetence.[60]

They have a point: hyperinflation like that in Venezuela, which reached 10 million percent a year in 2019,[61] can wipe out people's savings, make investors flee, and send the economy into a downward spiral.[62]

By taking the power to adjust the money supply out of the governments' hands, Bitcoin fans argue, Bitcoin can end inflation and the social ills that come with it.[63] The truth, though, is a lot more complicated, and Bitcoin might actually have the opposite problem.

The definition of inflation

First, let's step back and think about what inflation is in the first place. Inflation happens when the price of a basket of goods — say, a shopping cart full of groceries — increases. If a shopping cart full of groceries cost you $100 last year but now costs $105 (even with the exact same items inside), there was 5% inflation.[64h]

Inflation is a fact of life for most national economies; developed economies like the US typically average about 2% inflation a year.[65] This means the value of money slowly degrades over time. A $20 bill in 1919 was worth $300 in today's money, but today it's worth, well, $20.[66] An asset that once could have bought you dinner at a Michelin-starred restaurant[67] can now barely buy you a main course at the Cheesecake Factory.[68i]

Anyway, if you look carefully at the definition of inflation, you'll see that it presents a problem for Bitcoin. Inflation is calculated from the changing prices of physical goods — like a basket of groceries — over the years. Bitcoin's problem is that you can't really buy physical goods like groceries with bitcoins. A few stores let you buy physical items like mattresses with bitcoins,[69] but typically you aren't directly paying the merchant in bitcoins. Instead, your bitcoins are auto-converted to dollars (or whatever the local currency is), and the merchant is paid with those dollars.[70]

So you can't buy much with bitcoins besides other currencies. You could measure inflation using a "basket" of currencies: imagine you measured the number of bitcoins it would take to buy 100 US dollars, 100 euros, and 10,000 yen every year. The trouble is that

---

[h] In the United States, this is known as the *Consumer Price Index*, or *CPI*.
[i] We love the Cheesecake Factory, but it's no Michelin-star experience.

those currencies' values are always changing due to fluctuations in the foreign exchange markets and our old friend inflation.

So if the bitcoin price of that "basket" changed, you couldn't tell whether bitcoin or the currencies caused it. (Meanwhile, the "real" goods we usually put in our inflation-measuring basket have a fixed value; a box of cereal was just as useful ten years ago as it is today.) In short, the currency "basket" is a bad way to measure Bitcoin inflation, leaving you no good way to measure Bitcoin inflation at all.

The fans are right

For the sake of argument, let's leave that inconvenient fact aside and assume there *was* a world where people regularly bought and sold goods (like Hanyecz's pizzas) with nothing but bitcoins. Would Bitcoin suffer inflation in that world?

To Bitcoin fans' credit, the answer is most likely no. Inflation happens when the growth in the money supply outpaces the growth of the economy's GDP (the total value of goods and services sold in the economy).[71] If the money supply can't grow — which will effectively be the case for Bitcoin in a few decades — then inflation is mathematically impossible. (This definition raises yet another problem for Bitcoin: how do you measure the value of all goods and services bought with bitcoins? You can see details on all past Bitcoin transactions, but you have no way of knowing which transactions were for purchasing goods or services and which transactions were just gifting money to friends.)

It's worth noting, though, that the US dollar's inflation isn't as destructive as many Bitcoin proponents say. Bitcoin proponents are right that "governments continually print money, endlessly inflating the supply,"ʲ as one FAQ puts it.⁷² But it's not true that this printing "devalu[es] everyone's savings," as that FAQ continues. Nobody keeps their retirement savings in dollars. Instead, they put their money in stocks and bonds, which typically grow faster than inflation (the S&P 500 grows about 8% a year⁷³), making inflation not a significant problem for savers.

So, if you assume that you can measure Bitcoin's inflation in the first place, it's true that Bitcoin is immune to inflation, and if you take for granted that inflation is a bad thing, that's a win for Bitcoin. But Bitcoin is also very prone to the opposite problem: deflation.

Deflation

Deflation, as you might expect, happens when the price of a basket of goods declines over time: imagine if a basket of groceries cost $100 last year but just $95 this year.⁷⁴

If inflation happens when the money supply grows too quickly, deflation happens when the money supply grows too slowly or even shrinks.⁷⁵ This happened during the Great Depression: the money supply shrank due to a banking crisis,⁷⁶ leading to an average of 10% deflation a year between 1930 and 1933.⁷⁷

Shrinking supply

Bitcoin's money supply, as you'll recall, could quite possibly be decreasing. This is because it's so easy to lose bitcoins: lost or destroyed hard drives, bored investors, sending money to addresses that'll never spend them, and so on.

ʲ Note the sleight of hand here — growing the money supply doesn't always lead to inflation, though the sentence implies otherwise.

In fact, one 2020 study found that 10.7 million bitcoins (about 60% of all bitcoins ever mined at the time) hadn't been touched in a year and that 3.8 million bitcoins hadn't been touched in five years.[78] There's no way to tell how many of those coins are truly irreversibly lost; some of those unmoved coins are, no doubt, held by investors who are just sitting on them for the long term. But it's still problematic if even a fraction of those coins are gone forever.

Meanwhile, Bitcoin's periodic halvings mean that fewer and fewer bitcoins get mined over time. Only about 650,000 bitcoins were mined in 2019,[79] a figure that will shrink every four years. That means that Bitcoin's money supply is shrinking if more than 650,000 bitcoins are lost each year — which is quite possible, considering the staggering number of untouched bitcoins that that study found. And that money supply shortage would, per economic theory, lead to deflation. (Again, it's hard to measure Bitcoin's "deflation" due to the lack of a proper basket of goods, but we'll analyze it as best we can.)

Deflation would be good news for Bitcoin investors: with fewer bitcoins to go around, their coins would get scarcer and hence more valuable. But deflation isn't so healthy for the economy writ large. In a deflationary economy, your money gets more valuable over time, so there's plenty of incentive to hoard it and little incentive to invest or spend it.[80] This lines up perfectly with Bitcoin's *hodl*ing epidemic: people hold on to their bitcoins because they know each bitcoin's value is slowly increasing over time.[81]

The benefits of inflation

Capitalist economies need people to spend and invest money, though, since that's the only way the economy can grow. Deflation shuts this down. Meanwhile, a small, stable amount of inflation pushes people to invest — since they realize their money would become worthless if they sat on it forever — which helps keep the economy growing at a healthy rate.[82]

There are a few more technical reasons why economies need inflation. Here's one: imagine if there's an economic downturn and employers need to cut employees' wages. The problem is that employees don't like seeing their salary on paper decrease. When there's a little bit of inflation, employers can keep salaries constant, which keeps employees content but actually reduces the amount of goods they can buy with their salary. This means employers can effectively give employees a pay cut in economic rough patches, which helps the economy rebalance more quickly.[83]

(The salary you see on your paystub is called your *nominal wage*; *nominal* refers to dollar amounts. Meanwhile, the amount of stuff you can really buy with that salary is called your *real* wage; real quantities measure how many goods you can get for a certain amount of money, so they're ultimately more important for your standard of living.)[84]

If your economy has deflation, you miss out on the wheel-greasing benefits of small amounts of inflation, and your economy can grind to a halt if people hoard cash (or bitcoins) instead of trying to grow businesses.[85] So while Bitcoin's deflation may be a good thing for investors, who can see potentially massive returns by just holding (or *hodl*ing) coins, it would make Bitcoin a poor basis for a national (or world) economy.[86]

Investments or currency?

All this talk of inflation and deflation gets messy, since the terms don't really fit Bitcoin, but one thing is for sure: Bitcoin's value, in dollars, has grown over time.

This means that the buying power of a bitcoin has increased over time. Back in 2010, when a bitcoin was worth a fraction of a cent, it cost Hanyecz 10,000 bitcoins to buy a pizza. But nowadays, you'd only need a few thousandths of a bitcoin to buy a pizza. (Ten thousand bitcoins would probably be enough to buy a pizzeria or three.)

Stability vs. growth

In this way, Bitcoin behaves quite similarly to stocks, bonds, and other investments: they aim to increase in value over time. When Google went public in 2004, each share of stock was worth $85,[87] which is about $115 in today's money.[88] At the time of writing, each Google share is worth almost $1500.[89] Something that could once buy you just a GameBoy[90] can now buy you a MacBook.[91]

These assets stand in contrast to dollars, euros, and other currencies, which are mostly stable over time but gradually erode in value due to inflation. (Remember our story about the Michelin-starred restaurant and the Cheesecake Factory.)

This points to a key fact: the things that make an investment good are different than the things that make a currency good. Google stock is a great investment, but you would not want it to become the country's only legal tender, because commerce would become much harder. (Consumers wouldn't buy anything, since why buy something with shares today when you could wait a few months and, hopefully, be able to buy more with those same shares? And merchants would hesitate to accept it out of fear that its value could crash and they'd lose money.)

On the other hand, the US dollar is very stable, making it a great basis for transactions and the economy; you can trust that a dollar you spend or earn won't dramatically spike or crash in value. But investors don't make dollars the centerpiece of their investment strategy, since there's (by definition) no profit to be had and, indeed, inflation slowly eats away the value.

In other words, the thing that makes currencies good is stability, while the thing that makes investments good is growth. These are, of course, mutually exclusive. A financial instrument can't be both growing *and* stable at the same time.

US Dollar vs. investments over time

The US dollar's value is stable but slowly declining, while investments' values are volatile but grow in the long run. Bitcoin is, quite literally, off the charts, so we excluded it. Data source: Google Finance and Ian Webster[92]

Bitcoin: an investment through and through

Now, where does this leave Bitcoin?

Bitcoin is a strange financial instrument that is both a currency *and* an investment. You can use bitcoins to buy and sell things online, or you can buy and hold (or *hodl*) bitcoins in the hopes of turning a profit. Bitcoin is like Venmo (or PayPal), but if you sent and received stocks. This makes Bitcoin a truly unique financial invention.

But, as we just saw, a financial instrument can't be a good currency and a good investment at the same time; it has to choose one or the other. It's technically a currency, but it behaves much more like an investment.

If you look at Bitcoin's price over time, it's very clear that Bitcoin has chosen the investment path. Its value is famously volatile: it can drop[93] or surge[94] 20% in a single week. On one particularly frenzied day in December 2017, Bitcoin's price went from $15,000 in the morning to over $19,000 by lunchtime to about $16,000 by the late afternoon.[95] It remains unpredictable, but so far, it's grown tremendously in the long run.

These are all hallmarks of an investment, and indeed, Bitcoin's volatility and growth have been even more extreme than most stocks. While Wall Street calls it a sign of "extreme pessimism" if stocks fall 4% in a day[96] and a "bloodbath" when they fall 10% in a week,[97] such swings are small potatoes for Bitcoin, which is liable to gain[98] or shed[99] 10% of its value in a single day. But, of course, Bitcoin has the potential to create fortunes far faster than any stock can. (The consensus among investors is that investing in Bitcoin is like day-trading stocks: extremely risky, but with a huge potential for profit.[100])

It's even more instructive to look at the culture around Bitcoin. There's a whole cottage industry of experts analyzing the minute movements in Bitcoin's price to predict future price movements, borrowing in a slew of terms from Wall Street: *golden crosses*,[101] *Fibonacci retracements, cup and handle patterns, inverted heads and shoulders, AB=CD patterns, channel projections*,[102] and so on.

One Bitcoin analyst claimed to have found a "cup and handle" pattern in the price of Bitcoin. This pattern is considered a bullish signal, indicating future price growth.[103] Source: Vaido Veek[104]

These terms are common tools of the trade for *technical traders*, who seek to predict the price of a stock from just its past prices and trading volumes instead of analyzing the company, market, economy, and other fundamentals.[105] Fibonacci retracements, for instance, let you determine the short-term floor and ceiling (known as *support* and *resistance*, respectively) of a stock's price by dividing the distance between a recent price peak and valley by certain mathematical ratios derived from the Fibonacci sequence.[106]

And, of course, the times Bitcoin breaks into the news the most is when analysts believe Bitcoin's price will surge (or *moon*, in their parlance[107]). You've no doubt heard predictions that Bitcoin will hit $100,000[108] or even $1 million[109] a coin. And almost any news event, from threats of war[110] to virus outbreaks,[111] gets the speculators talking. In short, most of the chatter around Bitcoin is from investors and analysts like these, known as *crypto traders*,[112] who view Bitcoin as an investment and not a currency.

But perhaps the strongest evidence that Bitcoin users value it as an investment, not a currency, is to look at what happened when Bitcoin's price stayed in a narrow band between roughly $3600 to $4000 from December 2018 to March 2019.[113] If Bitcoin users really wanted Bitcoin to take off as a currency, they would have celebrated this unusual patch of price stability. People could finally make trades with bitcoins without worrying that their money would become useless or that they'd thrown away a source or profit.

But most people didn't celebrate that price stability. Instead, it was far more common to hear people saying that Bitcoin was "stuck"[114] or bemoaning that Bitcoin was being "rejected" and facing "resistance" as it tried to keep marching higher.[115] These are the words of profit-seeking investors, not people trying to replace our current monetary system.

So while Bitcoin can be both a currency and an investment, it's clearly chosen to be an investment. You can still use it as a currency, but it's highly flawed — and the things that make it such a flawed currency are the exact same things that make it such an interesting investment vehicle. Bitcoin may not be the future of money, but it may well be a part of the future of investing.

Chapter 3.

Bitcoin's Blunders

Bitcoin is an exciting new technology. For our Foundation work we are doing digital currency to help the poor get banking services. We don't use bitcoin specifically for two reasons. One is that the poor shouldn't have a currency whose value goes up and down a lot compared to their local currency. Second is that if a mistake is made in who you pay then you need to be able to reverse it so anonymity wouldn't work.

—Bill Gates, co-chair of the Bill and Melinda Gates Foundation[1]

I N HIS whitepaper, Satoshi described an elegant, mathematically-sound currency that truly let you make payments without a bank. But in the years since, Bitcoin has discovered that practice is much harder than theory, and we've seen that a lot of the utopian predictions that people made about the currency haven't quite panned out.

The scaling problem

As we saw last chapter, Bitcoin could be either a payment method or an investment vehicle, but it's morphed into primarily the latter. What makes this especially interesting is that Satoshi intended for Bitcoin to be the exact opposite.[2a]

When Satoshi announced Bitcoin on a cryptography-focused mailing list in 2008, the very first sentence of his announcement email read:

> *I've been working on a new electronic cash system that's fully peer-to-peer, with no trusted third party.*[3]

He didn't see Bitcoin as an alternative investment; he saw it as a payment system. The whole point was to "allow online payments to be sent directly from one party to another without going through a financial institution."[4]

Satoshi specifically called out smaller-value payments as a key use case for Bitcoin. In another mailing list post, he said:

> *Bitcoin is practical for smaller transactions than are practical with existing payment methods. Small enough to include what you might call the top of the micropayment range.*[5]

---

[a] Who was Satoshi? What did he believe? Read about it in Appendix C.

Satoshi didn't specify an exact dollar amount, but considering that *micropayments* are generally thought to be a few dollars or less,[6] let's assume he meant amounts between a few cents and a few dollars

Fees & delays

So, is Bitcoin an effective way to send, say, a dollar to someone else?

We already talked about how the volatility in Bitcoin's price — it's liable to fall[7] or jump[8] 20% in a single week — makes it a risky asset to pay or get paid with. But there's more to consider.

The biggest thing to consider is the fee. Remember that miners charge a fee on every transaction in a block. Each transaction specifies a fee it's willing to pay to get into a block and then goes to the *mempool* of all unconfirmed transactions.[9] Miners get to choose the transactions they put in their next block; you can imagine they'll choose the transactions that offer them the highest fees.

This means that, when there are more transactions vying for a spot in a block, transaction senders have to offer higher fees to win out. (It's like how Ubers and Lyfts cost a lot more during periods of peak demand, like right after New Year's.)

Note that the fee doesn't depend on how much money you're sending. The amount you're sending doesn't affect the transaction's size (in bytes),[10] and miners want to maximize the number of transactions they can fit in a block, so they don't care what's in your transaction, as long as you're paying well.

Anyway, the average fee was just a fraction of a cent back in Satoshi's and Hanyecz's days, but now that Bitcoin's price has risen and there's more interest in Bitcoin, the fee tends to hover between 50¢ and $1.[11] That's not terrible, especially if you're trying to move thousands of dollars. But if you're trying to send a dollar to a friend, like Satoshi envisioned, you definitely do not want to pay fees that high, especially when apps like Venmo let you send money for free.

The transaction crunch

The bigger problem with fees comes when there's a lot of congestion: when people are making transactions far faster than miners can bundle them into blocks (and remember that blocks can only be made every ten minutes), the increased demand will drive up the average fee.

Take December 2017 as a case study. The month marked the culmination of Bitcoin's year-long rally: the price of a bitcoin surged from under $1000 in January 2017 to over $19,000 at one point in December 2017. But this month, an unprecedented number of people were trying to buy and sell bitcoins, which led the average fee to spike — at one point, it was over $55.[12]

Bitcoin's average transaction fee over time

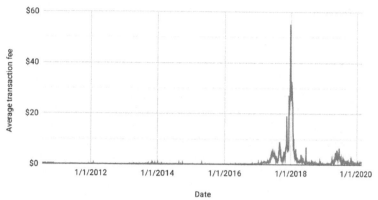

Bitcoin's transaction fees are usually less than a dollar, but they spike in times of high demand — the average fee surpassed $55 at one point. Data source: Bitinfocharts.com[13]

Another effect of the huge number of transactions was an excruciatingly long waiting time. At one point on December 7, 2017, the pool was full of over 200,000 unconfirmed transactions.[14] But since Bitcoin can only process a few thousand transactions an hour (12,000 to 15,000 an hour, at the time of writing[15]), the pool stayed congested for a long time. Around this time, it took an average of 16 hours for a transaction to get confirmed and put on the blockchain.[16] Imagine waiting at the counter for 16 hours waiting for your credit card to go through.

In short, Bitcoin struggled under this period of peak interest, when the culmination of the rally led to extreme delays and fees. A sufficiently motivated Bitcoin investor who was looking at profits of thousands of dollars could have overlooked the $55 fees and 16-hour waiting times, but someone trying to buy coffee would have found it inexcusable.

Unfortunately, this problem hasn't gone away. It's harder to get data on transaction waiting times, but fee spikes have become a common feature in Bitcoin rallies. When Bitcoin boomed in summer 2019, briefly surpassing $12,000 a coin in July 2019 after months under $4000, the fees saw a smaller but still substantial rise. From May to early July 2019, the fee was regularly over $2, topping $6 at one point.[17]

Fundamental problems

Bitcoin is poorly-suited to small payments in even the best case. Mike Hearn, a well-known early Bitcoin developer, estimated that Bitcoin could only handle about 3 transactions per second (abbreviated as *TPS*);[18] the latest data puts that figure at about 3.5 to 4 transactions a second.[19]

Meanwhile, Visa can handle vastly more transactions. It's hard to pin down an exact number — Morgan Stanley said that Visa and Mastercard combined could handle 5000 transactions per second,[20] Visa once bragged that it hit 11,000 transactions per second,[21] and a whitepaper estimated that Visa could max out at 45,000 transactions per second,[22] No matter the true number, Visa far surpasses Bitcoin's bandwidth.

And, while credit card transactions go through in seconds, Bitcoin transactions take an average of ten minutes to go through even if you offer a huge fee, since blocks are mined an average of ten minutes apart.[b] Merchants who accept Bitcoin are actually advised to wait for six *more* blocks to be mined after the transaction

---

[b] Blocks aren't mined every ten minutes on the dot; instead, there's a random chance that a block is mined every second. Blocks could be mined five seconds apart, or you could have to wait an hour between blocks, but it works out to an average of ten minutes per block. (This is known as a Poisson process.)

goes through to minimize the risk of fraud.[23] (Remember that an attacker with enough computing power could make a new chain and try to out-mine the main chain. The hope is that, once the main chain has mined six blocks, the attacker's chain will have fallen behind.) So the average processing time for a Bitcoin transaction can be up to an hour in even the best of circumstances!

In sum, while Bitcoin does avoid routing payments through a middleman, it comes at a steep cost: it's very inefficient for payments, especially the small payments that Satoshi hoped Bitcoin would be ideal for.

A scalable future?

That said, there's been some progress on trying to solve Bitcoin's inability to handle large amounts of payments, or, as it's known in Bitcoin circles, the *scaling problem*.

The foundational piece of Bitcoin's attempt to solve the scaling problem is *SegWit*, an optional upgrade to the Bitcoin *protocol* (the rules around how bitcoins are created, stored, and spent)[24] that Bitcoin users, miners, and exchanges could switch to.[25]

SegWit, which became officially activated in September 2017, moves certain metadata about each transaction (including the signature that proves who sent the transaction) to a new part of the block, which frees up more room in the body of the block for transactions.[26]

This lets more transactions fit inside a block and thus increases Bitcoin's total transactions-per-second. (The name SegWit is an abbreviation of "segregated witness;" the metadata with the signature is called the "witness," and it's "segregated" away from the main transaction data.[27])

Another well-known potential solution is called the Lightning Network, which aims to do most transactions "off the blockchain" to avoid the fees and delays of transactions put on the blockchain. Each pair of people tracks their payments to each other on a digital scratchpad; they only "settle" their balances once in a while.[28]

Imagine if you and a friend went on vacation together. The Lightning approach would be to track all the times one of you paid for the other in a spreadsheet and "settle up" with a single payment at the end of the trip, instead of you paying each other back after every single meal, hotel booking, train ticket, and so on.

Criminals' favorite currency

For the first few years of its existence, Bitcoin was commonly associated with shadowy e-criminals; people knew it as that mysterious currency used by drug lords and hackers. And, truth be told, it lived up to that reputation.

The Silk Road

The most famous criminal enterprise built on Bitcoin was the Silk Road, a sort of Amazon for the illegal. From 2011 to 2013,[29] the Silk Road sold everything from drugs to fake passports,[30] moving over $1.2 billion in contraband over its short existence.[31] (To the Silk Road's credit, some items were banned. The website's founder, an American programmer named Ross Ulbricht, only allowed goods that led to "victimless crimes," in his words. This meant that assassinations, stolen credit card numbers, and child pornography — things that directly hurt another human — were banned.[32])

As you can imagine, contraband buyers and sellers didn't want to leave a paper trail by paying with credit cards. They turned to the still-young Bitcoin as the primary mode of payment for the site.[33]

The relative anonymity offered by Bitcoin doubtlessly frustrated law enforcement's attempts to track down the criminal activity on the site.

The party didn't last forever. In 2013, FBI agents tracked down Ulbricht, known to the world as the Dread Pirate Roberts,[c] to a library in San Francisco, while he was logged into the Silk Road on his laptop.[34] After dramatically arresting Ulbricht, the authorities seized the server that ran the Silk Road, shuttering the site for good.[35d]

Darker markets

But the Silk Road wasn't even the worst of them. A website named Cthulhu let you hire hitmen, offering the services of "an organized criminal group" of former soldiers and mercenaries.[36e]

And, ever since the Silk Road, there have been entire forums and online stores dedicated to selling stolen credit card numbers, a practice known as *carding*.[37] The security researcher Brian Krebs published a well-known tour of a "carding" shop known as McDumpals, whose logo is Ronald McDonald pointing a gun at the viewer.[38]

The currency of choice for all these criminal enterprises? Bitcoin. As Cthulhu put it, the advantage of Bitcoin was that "we don't know you and you don't know you," so "we can't send you to prison, and you can't send us to prison."[39] (The underbelly of the internet really is terrifying.)

---

[c] The name of a character from the ever-quotable movie The Princess Bride.

[d] Ulbricht fell victim to one of the classic blunders, the most famous of which is, "never get involved in a Bitcoin scheme in San Francisco."

[e] Their tagline: "Solutions to Common Problems!" Charming.

Hackers

It's not just illicit merchants that love Bitcoin; hackers are fond of the mostly-anonymous currency as well.

The most visible example of hackers using Bitcoin is with *ransomware*, a type of malware or computer virus that infects a computer, encrypts all the files, and threatens to throw away the key unless the user sends a "ransom" of bitcoins to a particular address.[40] In other words: pay up or kiss your documents goodbye.

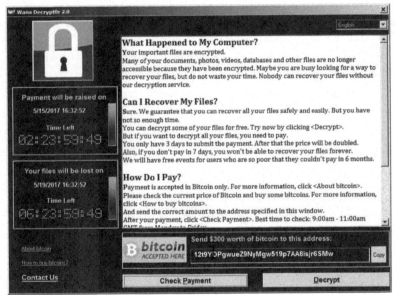

A screen shown to victims of the WannaCry ransomware, which crippled organizations ranging from hospitals[41] to car manufacturers.[42] The hackers demanded $300 in Bitcoin to decrypt users' files. Source: Wikimedia [43]

Ransomware burst into the news after the emergence of the WannaCry strain of ransomware, which infected Windows computers around the world in 2017.[44] As expected, the hackers demanded payment in Bitcoin to cover their tracks.

Ironically, though, Bitcoin wasn't a great choice for them. By May 2017, the WannaCry hackers only made about $50,000 in ransom despite infecting 200,000 computers, or 40¢ a computer. This feeble haul was due in large part to the fact that many of their victims weren't tech-savvy enough to know where to buy bitcoins, how to get them, and how to transfer them to the hackers.[45] (The people most likely to fall victim to the ransomware were probably the least tech-savvy; why did the hackers expect them to be able to negotiate the confusing world of Bitcoin?)

What's more, journalists found the Bitcoin addresses of some of the masterminds behind the WannaCry attack, and the general public (not to mention law enforcement) could watch as money flowed in. (Quartz observed that the address

12t9YDPgwueZ9NyMgw519p7AA8isjr6SMw

got 38 ransom payments.)[46]

Because all transfers of money in or out of those addresses could be seen publicly, the hackers would have had that much harder a time trying to use their ill-gotten gains. Indeed, journalists noticed when over $140,000 of bitcoins were moved out of the hackers' wallets in August 2017.[47]

And finally, there were signs that Bitcoin was too volatile for even the WannaCry hackers.[48] They demanded first $300, and later $600, in Bitcoin from their victims.[49] Note that they didn't request bitcoins, but rather a dollar amount that the victims would have to convert to Bitcoin.

Liberty Reserve

An interesting conclusion to this saga: Bitcoin wasn't the first digital currency that cybercriminals used. It's not clear which one was the first,[50] but the most prominent such currency before Bitcoin was Liberty Reserve, a little-known illicit payment processor that operated out of Costa Rica from 2006 to 2013.[51]

Liberty Reserve was both shadier and simpler than Bitcoin. Users would work with a middleman in countries like Malaysia, Nigeria, or Vietnam to deposit money into a Liberty Reserve bank account in Costa Rica. Users could then move money around freely to other Liberty Reserve users. And then users could work with other money exchangers to withdraw money from their Liberty Reserve accounts.[52]

Costa Rica had almost no financial oversight of Liberty Reserve,[53] and the use of middlemen ensured that Liberty Reserve had no idea who was really operating the bank accounts,[54] so Liberty Reserve was essentially an anonymous way to launder money and pay for illicit goods while flying under the radar of the authorities. Nobody would know what you were spending money on, nobody would know who you were transacting with, and nobody would know where your profits came from.

As you might expect, Liberty Reserve was a hit with drug traffickers, credit card thieves, hackers, and all the other usual suspects.[55]

Leaving aside the obvious criminality, Liberty Reserve is an interesting case study for us. Unlike Bitcoin, it was highly centralized, using a shady web of extralegal communication channels to avoid scrutiny. And unlike Bitcoin, it was explicitly a payment method, not a store of value: each "LR dollar" was worth exactly one US dollar, so you'd earn no profit from holding on to it.[56] This shows that the actual mechanics of a currency don't matter that much; as long as it's relatively anonymous, criminals will abuse it.

That is unfortunate, because there are people who would legitimately benefit from anonymous currencies. Imagine a dissident in an authoritarian regime who doesn't want their digital payments being tracked. But if criminals are the #1 customers of anonymous currencies, you have to wonder if it's worth it.

Not quite anonymous

There's a reason that we've been calling Bitcoin "mostly anonymous" so far: it isn't anonymous. It's true that your name isn't directly attached to your Bitcoin transactions, but your Bitcoin addresses are, and your identity can be connected to your addresses if your opponents are sufficiently motivated. That is, Bitcoin is *pseudonymous*, and your pseudonym can be broken more easily than you might think.

To illustrate this, it's instructive to revisit our old friend Ross Ulbricht, who owned the Silk Road.

After FBI agents arrested Ulbricht in San Francisco, Ulbricht's lawyer claimed he had been framed and wasn't really the Dread Pirate Roberts, the shadowy owner of the Silk Road. So the FBI went back to Ulbricht's seized laptop and found the addresses of his Bitcoin wallets on his hard drive. They already knew the addresses of the Silk Road's wallets, where money earned from fees on the site was stored. [57]

All the agents had to do was look on the Bitcoin blockchain for transactions between the Silk Road's addresses and Ulbricht's addresses, and voilà: they found over 3700 transactions between the Silk Road and Ulbricht, which together moved over 700,000 bitcoins.[58] There was no longer any doubt that Ulbricht was the Dread Pirate Roberts.[f]

Most people wouldn't shed tears over Ulbricht's fate, but the key point remains: the remarkable transparency of Bitcoin's blockchain makes Bitcoin far less anonymous than its supporters might make it out to be.

The Mt. Gox hack

Bitcoin prides itself on its security, and it's largely correct. It would take a supercomputer millions of years to crack the one-way hash functions that Bitcoin uses for mining and address generation,[59] making it nearly impossible for someone to cheat the mining algorithm or guess your private key. And, due to the proof-of-work system, it's nearly impossible to forge past transactions outside of a 51% attack.[60]

But one place where Bitcoin's security promises fall short is that it's as vulnerable to human error as any other technology. The most famous example of this shortfall is the story of the downfall of Mt. Gox, once the world's premier Bitcoin exchange.[61]

Founded in 2010 in Tokyo, Mt. Gox let people around the world exchange government-issued, or *fiat*, currencies like dollars and yen for bitcoins and vice versa.[62] (Mt. Gox actually began life in 2009 as an exchange for trading cards from the game *Magic: The Gathering*. The name "Mt. Gox" comes from "*Magic: The Gathering Online Exchange.*" The site quickly pivoted to Bitcoin.[63]) Mt. Gox grew quickly, and by 2013, over 70% of the world's Bitcoin trading flowed through the platform.[64]

---

[f] Another classic blunder: never go in against a blockchain when jail time is on the line.

Mt. Gox suffered a few hacking scares and brushes with the US Department of Homeland Security, but overall, business was booming until early 2014.[65]

One day in February 2014, Mt. Gox suddenly halted all withdrawals of money from the exchange, preventing traders from liquidating any bitcoins in their Mt. Gox wallets and getting fiat currencies out.[66] A few weeks later, Mt. Gox shut down all trading on the site.[67] Just a few days after that, Mt. Gox filed for bankruptcy.[68] Eight hundred and fifty thousand bitcoins,[69] then worth $450 million[70] and at the time of writing worth over $8 billion,[71] disappeared without a trace.

Mt. Gox had gone from towering peak to smoldering crater in less than a month. It was called the "Lehman Brothers of blockchain."[72] What happened?

The theft

It turns out that Mt. Gox's troubles had, unbeknownst to most of its users, begun as early as 2011. Mt. Gox stored users' account balances in particular wallets — *wallet* just being a term for a private key and address pair. In 2011, an attacker — either a hacker or a rogue employee — copied a file called "wallet.dat" from Mt. Gox's servers; this file contained the private keys to Mt. Gox's wallets.[73]

Over the next few years, the attacker, now armed with Mt. Gox's private keys, slowly drained the wallets of their bitcoins. Mt. Gox was totally unaware of the theft. In fact, it thought that the attacker siphoning funds from Mt. Gox's wallets was just a customer depositing money into their account.[74] Bizarrely, Mt. Gox even credited other customers 40,000 bitcoins, apparently thinking that they were making deposits connected to this thief's "deposits."[75]

It's not clear exactly how many coins the thief stole from Mt. Gox. Two hundred thousand of the 850,000 coins were later found, but about 600,000 remain unaccounted for. Some believe that Mt. Gox never held that many coins to begin with and cooked the books to make Mt. Gox seem in better financial shape than it really was.[76]

Security specialists eventually identified a Russian man named Alexander Vinnik as the owner of the wallets that the stolen funds were moved into. Vinnik was the owner of a shady rival Bitcoin exchange, BTC-e;[77] about 300,000 of those stolen coins had been sold on BTC-e.[78]

When news of the colossal theft reached the press, the Bitcoin world panicked, and Bitcoin's price plunged 20%.[79] Some even feared it would be "the end of Bitcoin."[80]

The lesson

The theft clearly wasn't the end of Bitcoin, but it did reveal how Bitcoin — for all its technological sophistication — doesn't guard against shoddy security practices. A Bitcoin wallet is only as secure as its private key, and if someone gets ahold of that private key, the money is theirs — and if they steal it, it's practically irreversible.[g]

Mt. Gox was, indeed, infamous for its shoddy security practices and unprofessional business operations in general.[81] It didn't test new code before it launched the code to customers, meaning that customers could easily run into bugs that broke their accounts. It

---

[g] The only way to undo that theft is to make a "fork" of the blockchain that erases that theft from history. But then you have a whole new currency, and getting people to join a new currency is always a challenge. We'll see how another cryptocurrency used this tactic later in the book.

kept no backups of its source code, meaning that there was no way to roll back a mistaken code change. It only let one person approve code changes, and that person was Mt. Gox's CEO, Mark Karpeles. [82]

It didn't help that Karpeles paid little attention to the details of the business, preferring to spend his time — and millions of dollars — on a pet project called the Bitcoin Cafe, a shop in Tokyo where you would be able to buy drinks with Bitcoin. Karpeles was lax in approving code; even critical security fixes took weeks to get approved and roll out.[83]

But Mt. Gox's inexcusable slip-up was storing private keys unencrypted on a shared server.[84] Private keys are usually *encrypted* before they're stored; you need to enter a special *decryption key* before you can access the private key, otherwise the private key will just look like gibberish. Had Mt. Gox encrypted the wallet.dat file, the attacker wouldn't have been able to extract the private keys. But by keeping the file unencrypted — or in *cleartext*[85] — Mt. Gox set itself up for this attack.

All this goes to show that crypto-institutions like Mt. Gox aren't necessarily any more secure than regular institutions. Anyone with poor security practices can get hacked, blockchain or no blockchain.

The alternative

That said, the Bitcoin community has discovered techniques to avoid such hacks from happening again. The most notable such technique is called *cold storage*, which stores private keys away from an internet-connected computer,[86] thus ensuring that no cyberthief can steal it.

Cold storage takes one of two common forms. The first is a *paper wallet*, where private keys and addresses are printed on a piece of paper and kept in a safe place. [87] It's not too different from keeping your bank password written on a sticky note in your study: it's inconvenient to use and easy to misplace, but it ensures that no hacker on the internet can get their hands on it.

An example paper wallet. The code on the far left is the address, and the code on the far right is a private key. Scannable QR codes save you the pain of typing in the entire private key and address. Source: BitcoinPaperWallet[88]

The other form of cold storage is a USB stick that stores your private key, called a *hardware wallet*. It's secure because your private key lives on the USB stick and never leaves it; transactions are signed on the private key, so you can send money without your (internet-connected) computer ever seeing your private key. [89]

What's more, some hardware wallets make you press a physical button to approve sending money,[90] thus making it impossible for an attacker to take your money unless they can get your hardware wallet. The strategy of having a physical item to supplement a digital login has gotten quite common in tech; if you've ever used *two-factor authentication* like approving a login with your phone, you've used this approach.

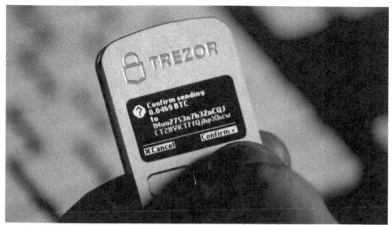

A hardware wallet. Your private keys stay on this small device, which plugs into your computer via the USB port. You need to use physical buttons to approve a transaction. Source: Wikimedia[91]

The somewhat paradoxical theory behind cold storage is that it's actually safer to store sensitive things offline, since anything stored on an internet-connected computer can be found by a motivated-enough hacker. Cold storage would certainly have helped Mt. Gox, since the hacker would have had to physically break into Mt. Gox headquarters (or rob the CEO) to steal the money instead of quietly siphoning money away from a safe distance.

Cold storage is still a bit inconvenient to use, though. For that reason, experts say that the best approach is to keep long-term savings in cold storage and keep money for daily expenses in a normal internet-connected computer, [92] known as *hot storage.* [93]

Mining and climate change

Alex Hern of the Guardian summed up Bitcoin's proof-of-work mining algorithm well: "Bitcoin mining is a competition to waste the most electricity possible by doing pointless arithmetic quintillions of times a second."[94]

The wastefulness of mining does serve a purpose — keeping Bitcoin tamper-proof — but Hern is still right that it's wasteful, and the competition is getting more extreme each passing day. Miners are locked in a perpetual arms race. Your chance of successfully mining a block is proportional to the percent of total hash power you control, so if other miners build more powerful mining computers (known in mining slang as *rigs*[95]), you have to build more powerful rigs yourself just to keep up.

This arms race moves astoundingly quickly. A mining rig that could churn out 1 trillion hashes a second, or 1 TH/s, would have earned you about $20,000 a day in early 2011; that same rig would have earned you just $4 a day in early 2015 and just 10¢ a day in early 2020.[96] (These rigs take a lot of electricity, and electricity costs money, so it's quite likely you would have been operating at a loss in early 2020.)

Because beefier rigs — those that can power through more hashes per second — take more energy, Bitcoin's energy use is steadily increasing, and the trend doesn't appear to be slowing anytime soon. The University of Cambridge estimates that Bitcoin's annual energy consumption skyrocketed from about 6 terawatt-hours (roughly the annual power consumption of Luxembourg) in 2017 to over 80 terawatt-hours (roughly the annual power consumption of Finland) in 2020.[97]

Bitcoin's energy consumption vs. countries and states

Bitcoin now uses more energy per year than many countries and US states. Data source: University of Cambridge[98] and US Energy Information Administration[99]

That 80 terawatt-hour figure is more than 185 of the 219 countries in the CIA's database,[100] including Switzerland, Greece, Israel, Singapore, Portugal, Peru, and New Zealand. And it's more than the annual electricity usage of 34 US states (plus DC).[101h]

And, according to one estimate, the mining work required to verify a single Bitcoin transaction uses enough electricity to power an average American household for 22 days, generates the same carbon footprint as over 750,000 Visa transactions (that's 300 kilograms of carbon dioxide), and generates two golf balls' worth of e-waste.[102i]

---

h Using the "Total Retail Sales" metric.

i Of course, miners don't verify transactions individually; the stats cited here represent the total outputs of mining a block divided by the average number of transactions per block.

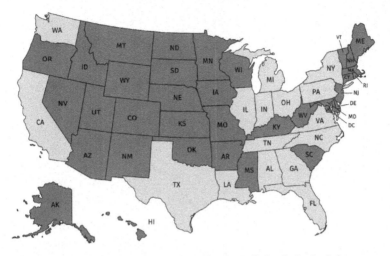

Bitcoin mining uses more energy annually than all the dark-shaded states. Data source: US Energy Information Administration[103]. Map made with Mapchart.net.[104]

Suffice it to say that Bitcoin is using a rapidly-increasing amount of energy at a time when humanity needs to cut back its energy use to stave off the worst effects of climate change,[105] and it's generating huge amounts of carbon when we need to be reducing our carbon footprint.

It's somewhat heartening to hear that, per one report, 80% of all Bitcoin mining uses renewable energy,[106] but still, using excessive energy — of any form — is worrisome.

The myth of the solo miner

The early days of Bitcoin were truly like California in the Gold Rush days of the 1840's and 1850's. Any hobbyist with a powerful homemade computer, or even a solid laptop, could make tens or hundreds of dollars a day by mining Bitcoin.[107] By our estimates, even as late as 2013, you could make $5-10 a day by mining with a lowly MacBook.[108][109][j] Students even kicked around the idea of using school computers to mine.[110]

Few people made it filthy rich off Bitcoin mining[111] (early investors tended to do better), but still, it was easy money. And that was a key selling point for Bitcoin: with many small, independent miners competing, nobody would be able to amass enough power to out-mine the main chain and thus forge transactions with the 51% attack we discussed earlier[112]. And the idea of self-sufficient, "small business" owners making money without help from the government or big corporations fit with Bitcoin's libertarian ethos.[113]

But that myth — of a solo miner, laptop or homemade rig in hand, striking it rich — has long since evaporated.

Arms race

The fundamental problem is that Bitcoin mining has gotten prohibitively competitive. The number of blocks you can mine is proportional to the fraction of the world's total hash power you control, so your key to making more money is to build more powerful computers than your competitors. Since everyone thinks that way, everyone builds more powerful computers — but that just leaves everyone back at the same competitive position they were at before.[114]

Indeed, the total hash power of the Bitcoin *network*, the term for the entire ecosystem of miners, has skyrocketed over time:

---

[j] Like before, we're estimating that a MacBook can do one billion hashes per second, or 1 GH/s.

Bitcoin network's total hash rate over time

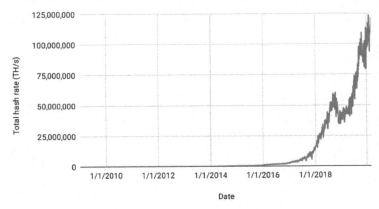

The Bitcoin network's total hash rate (also known as the total hash power), which is the sum of all miners' hash rates. It's exploded in recent years because everyone's. Data source: Blockchain.com[115]

Interestingly, in Bitcoin's early days, Satoshi urged miners to follow a "gentlemen's agreement" to not use extremely powerful computers to mine,[116] showing that he must have known of the destructive potential for an arms race. Clearly, though, that agreement didn't last long; the potential to defect and earn gobs of money must have proven too tempting to miners.

Massive investments

Since the network's total hash power is so high, a miner needs to command a huge amount of hash power themselves to stand a competitive chance of mining a block.

Laptops are no longer good enough to mine; a MacBook would mine over 50,000 times slower[117] than that $2000 mining rig we mentioned earlier.[118] You'd also burn out your laptop in the process.[119]

So, practically, the only way to be an independent miner these days is to invest thousands of dollars in an ASIC-powered mining computer, also known as a *mining rig*. The trouble is that, even with that $2000 rig, it would take you about 38 years, on average, to mine a block. [120k]

You would earn a king's ransom for actually mining a block — the block reward is 12.5 bitcoins, over $110,000, at the time of writing[121] — but, until you got a block, you'd be spending decades waiting on a machine that can do literally nothing besides mine.[122] Oh, and that expensive computer will add about $2000 a year to your electricity bill.[123]

The other problem is that, as the arms race continues, you have to keep upgrading your equipment to stay competitive:

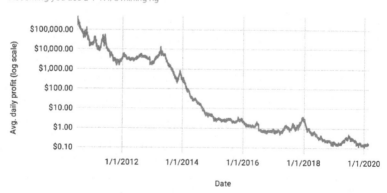

Bitcoin mining profitability over time

Assuming you use a 1 TH/s mining rig

The profitability of any mining rig will drastically decline over time as the arms race continues; you'll need to keep getting beefier rigs to earn a decent income. Data source: Bitinfocharts.com[124]

---

[k] Like before, assuming Bitcoin's difficulty score is 15.5 trillion (as it is at the time of writing).

In short, solo miners have no chance of earning money from Bitcoin mining unless they consistently invest large amounts of money in specialized equipment. At that rate, they might just be better off just buying bitcoins off an exchange and hoping for the best.

Mining pools

One quick fix to the randomness of payouts is to join a *mining pool*, or a club of miners who share their hash power and split the proceeds from any blocks they mine.[125] A sufficiently large pool will mine blocks at pretty regular intervals, so you'll earn a regular income proportional to the amount of computing power you contribute to the pool.[126]

Mining pools don't increase your expected earnings; you actually lose money in the long run because the pools take a 1-3% fee on all mining rewards.[127] But it does smooth out your earnings, which is helpful; most people would rather earn, say, $100 every year than have a 1% chance of winning $10,000 each year.

Cloud mining

Mining pools still require you to have your own hardware, which has a high upfront cost. One newer alternative for more casual miners is *cloud mining*: you just rent mining rigs from a professional and collect a portion of the profits from whatever blocks your rented rigs mine. The company that runs the cloud rigs takes care of buying, maintaining, and upgrading the computers.[128]

It is indeed quite like cloud computing, where you rent storage space and computing power from a specialized service like Amazon Web Services (AWS) or Microsoft Azure instead of trying to run servers yourself.[129] (In case you're wondering, AWS frowns upon customers using rented servers to mine Bitcoin.[130])

Besides the lower barrier to entry,[131] this approach comes with many cost savings. For one, cloud mining can be very efficient because it benefits from economies of scale. Instead of setting up a bunch of small rigs, cloud mining tends to build giant *mining farms*, huge setups with tens or hundreds of ASIC-powered mining rigs all mining together.[132] This lets them average out the high fixed costs of cooling, security, and storage.

A Bitcoin mining farm, full of hundreds of ASIC-powered mining rigs that do nothing but mine all day. Source: Wikimedia[133]

Cloud mining also lets you outsource mining to more favorable parts of the world. The biggest cost in mining comes from electricity;[134] unfortunately for miners, the high-tech hubs where Bitcoin enthusiasts gather also tend to have the highest costs of electricity.[135] Keeping the energy-sucking mining rigs cool is another major challenge. And finally, having a strong internet is essential because every second your rig is offline is a second you're not mining.[136]

Thus, places with cheap electricity, cold weather, and fast internet (in roughly decreasing order of importance) are great for mining.[137] China has dirt-cheap coal power[138] and ever-increasing internet access, making it the most popular place to mine: by one estimate, 80% of all bitcoins are mined in China.[139]

Colder, northern locales are very popular for cloud mining as well: Iceland for its abundant (and cheap!) geothermal energy,[140] Quebec for its plentiful hydroelectric power (it's two to three times cheaper than the rest of North America), and Russia for its cheap nuclear and hydroelectric power.[141] Cloud miners started using so much electricity in Quebec, in fact, that the province temporarily stopped selling power to miners in 2018 because they needed to save some power for actual Quebec residents.[142]

A geothermal power plant in Iceland, which generates electricity from underground hot spots. Bitcoin miners love mining in Iceland because geothermal power is so cheap and plentiful. Source: Wikimedia[143]

The biggest downside to cloud mining is that a lot of the firms that offer these services are fraudulent: they sell you long-term subscriptions, operate for a few months, and then shut down operations and run. Other cloud mining businesses, many of which are registered anonymously under fake addresses, offer suspiciously high "commissions" for referring new customers;[144] well-known Bitcoin developer Gavin Andresen went after these shady businesses, arguing that "many will turn out to be Ponzi schemes."[145]

The other problem comes from simple economics. Because there's virtually zero barrier to entry — anyone can sign up to cloud mine with a click — people will keep joining until all the profit is sucked out of cloud mining. If cloud mining becomes profitable again, more people will join until competition becomes so high that it becomes unprofitable for everyone. (This is a textbook example of a *perfectly competitive market*: in these markets, where there's no barrier to entry, there are no profits in the long run.[146]) At the time of writing, you can still eke out a profit if you find a cloud mining firm with low electricity costs,[147] but we wonder how long that'll last.

Pickaxe theory

Even with tools like mining pools and cloud mining, Bitcoin mining isn't a very profitable venture for small-time, solo miners anymore. Perhaps the best way to make money off Bitcoin mining is to take a page from entrepreneurs in the original Gold Rush.

Gold fever struck California after gold was discovered in Sutter's Mill, not far from Sacramento. Young men from around the United States and the world flocked to the state in the hopes of striking it rich.[148] But there wasn't much hope for these aspiring miners: conditions were tough, earnings steadily decreased as competition increased,[149] and equipment was so expensive (new boots cost $2500 in today's dollars)[150] that there wasn't much chance of making money.[1]

Sutter's Mill in California, where the discovery of gold in 1848 sparked the California Gold Rush. Source: California Department of Parks and Recreation[151]

No, the real money to be made in the Gold Rush was by selling goods to the miners.[152] Samuel Brannan, a merchant from New York, set up a general store in Sutter's Mill[153] and quickly became rich by selling wheelbarrows, tents, and, yes, pickaxes to miners.[154] (He stimulated demand by running around the streets of San Francisco, waving a bottle of gold dust, which led even more men to swarm the gold mines.[155m]) Before long, Brannan was the wealthiest man in California.[156]

Even more famous than Brannan was a German immigrant named Levi Strauss, who made his fortune selling clothing and

---

[1] Sounds a lot like the evolution of Bitcoin mining.
[m] San Francisco's Brannan Street, incidentally, is home to many startup offices.

fabric to miners. (His famous blue jeans were not invented until the 1870s, well after the Gold Rush.)[157]

Entrepreneurs in today's Silicon Valley, which isn't all that different from the California of the gold-rush days, have taken that lesson to heart. The popular *pickaxe theory* argues that it's hard to get rich by participating in the latest technological craze — but it's very profitable to sell equipment to those who are. While it's unlikely that you'd get lucky enough to hit gold, it's a sure bet that a lot of people will be trying to cash in on the fad, and they're very eager to buy equipment.[158]

The same lesson applies to Bitcoin. While miners aren't making much real profit, mining mania is pushing up the price of *GPUs*,[159] which are computer chips normally used to render computer graphics for video games and 3D animated movies, generate scientific models, and do other computationally-heavy heavy tasks.[160] GPUs are often used as cheaper, but less effective, versions of ASICs, so they're a hit among low-budget miners or gamers trying to make some extra cash.[161] The American GPU manufacturers AMD and Nvidia have seen their stock prices surge as miners for Bitcoin and other cryptocurrencies have snapped up their chips.[162n] By one estimate, miners bought 3 million GPUs, totaling over $750 million, in 2017.[163]

Other companies have gotten shockingly rich off ASICs. The most famous is Bitmain, a Chinese that started off selling their Antminer line of ASIC-powered mining rigs. Bitmain now controls 70-80% of the Bitcoin mining hardware market.[164] Bitmain became so

---

[n] Even the best GPUs are still thousands or millions of times worse at Bitcoin mining than ASICs, so we think the craze isn't justified. Later on, though, we'll meet some smaller cryptocurrencies that are *ASIC-resistant*, meaning that GPUs are actually the best way to mine them.

flush with cash that it has since branched out into running a cloud mining firm[165] and mining pools. Its two largest mining pools, AntPool and BTC.com, once owned almost half of the world's mining power.[166]

So, if you're a small-time entrepreneur hoping to cash in on the Bitcoin craze, your best strategy may not be to get your hands dirty mining — you may well want to sell digital pickaxes.

Centralization

That last story about Bitmain's remarkable power may well concern you, and it probably would concern Satoshi, whoever and wherever he is.°

This is because the founding principle of Bitcoin, and the central philosophy of the crypto-libertarian community that has sprung up around the currency, is decentralization. It's the idea that individuals should have total control over their funds, without any interference from governments (and, presumably, big corporations). No government or bank should be able to control the direction Bitcoin;[167] the currency should be tearing down existing power structures, not reinforcing them.[168]

But the Bitcoin world has been trending more and more toward centralization in recent years. A few major players are gobbling up parts of Bitcoin's essential infrastructure, and it's getting harder for an individual (especially one who's not rich) to have a say on the future of the currency.

° We discuss who Satoshi is, and what he may believe in, in Appendix C.

Few nodes

Bitcoin's blockchain is huge: at the time of writing, it's over 250 GB and packing on about 50 GB a year.[169] This makes it too big to fit on many laptops,[170] and even on laptops that can fit something that huge, it's a massive use of space that could be going toward photos, documents, games, and other files that you probably value more than millions of old transactions. And that's not to mention that your phone would have an even harder time storing that much data.

Bitcoin's blockchain size over time

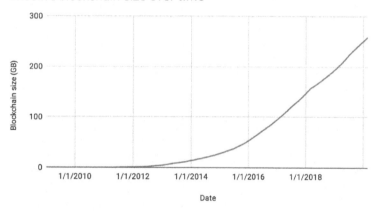

Bitcoin's blockchain has steadily swelled in size as more and more transactions have been made. Data source: Blockchain.com[171]

For this reason, most Bitcoin users don't store the entire blockchain on their devices. Instead, they only store a partial copy of the blockchain on their devices, making them what are known as *lightweight nodes*. They rely on other people to run *full nodes*, or computers that store the entire blockchain, to validate transactions and make sure they have the latest blocks on the blockchain.[172] The tradeoff is that people with lightweight nodes can't be 100% sure that all the transactions they're getting are legitimate; they have to trust the owners of the full nodes.

The problem is that nobody gets paid to maintain a full node, yet full nodes are essential for Bitcoin to operate since they're the only ones that store the official blockchain. Experts say that the lack of a financial incentive and the mounting difficulty of maintaining a full node mean average Bitcoiners will no longer maintain full nodes. Instead, it'll fall on a few huge companies that profit massively from Bitcoin — mining pools, ASIC manufacturers like Bitmain, cloud mining firms, et al. — to run full nodes.[173]

It's hard to know exactly who's running the nodes, but it's already clear that the number of nodes is stagnating despite ever-growing interest in Bitcoin. At the time of writing, the number of Bitcoin full nodes hasn't budged from about 10,000 in the last two years.[174]

Bitcoin full nodes over time

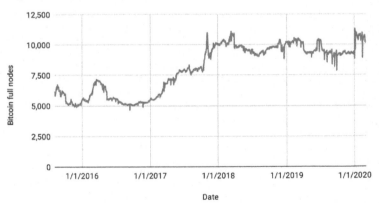

The total number of Bitcoin full nodes — computers that store the full blockchain — has flatlined since 2018. Data source: CoinDance[175]

If those experts are right, a few powerful entities will indeed control the future of the blockchain — and hence the currency.

Same software

The second case of Bitcoin's troubling centralization is with the software that runs on full nodes, known as *Bitcoin clients* or *implementations*. At the time of writing, 97.5% of all full nodes run the Bitcoin Core client software — that's 10,341 nodes out of 10,605. The second-place client, Bitcore, only runs on 111 nodes.[176]

It wasn't always this way; other clients used to put up a fight. Bitcoin XT ran on over 1000 full nodes in 2015 — over 15% of all full nodes at the time. Bitcoin Classic ran on over 2000 full nodes at its peak in 2016 — over 30% of all full nodes. But at the time of writing, there are just 2 nodes running Bitcoin XT and 3 running Bitcoin Classic. Bitcoin Core hasn't had any serious competition since early 2018, when Bitcoin Unlimited collapsed.[177]

Bitcoin clients' market share over time

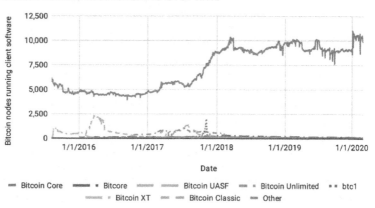

The market for Bitcoin client software used to be fairly competitive, but Bitcoin Core has long since vanquished its rivals. Data source: CoinDance[178]

Looking at the graph, you'll notice that the number of Bitcoin Core full nodes flatlined as soon as Bitcoin Unlimited collapsed.

It's hard to infer causality from this, but it's troubling that Bitcoin Core stopped expanding as soon as it defeated its last rival. That's what you usually expect from monopolies.

The dominance of a single piece of software isn't necessarily a bad thing. But, disturbingly, the team behind Bitcoin Core is primarily funded by a blockchain company called Blockstream.[179] And, more disturbingly, Blockstream employs a large number of the core Bitcoin Core team.[180]

And while Bitcoin Core says that it has a large and thriving community of programmers,[181] *The Verge* reports that Bitcoin Core's code is so complicated, and the dangers of getting something wrong so high, that only a handful of programmers can actually understand the full system and implement changes.[182]

This should worry any proponent of decentralization: the software that's at the heart of Bitcoin is primarily owned and maintained by a small group of people that are employed and funded by a single company. The potential for conflicts of interest and user-hostile changes by Blockstream is high.

Few mining pools

Mining independently, as we mentioned before, isn't a very sustainable way to make money. So it should be no surprise that mining pools are the most common — and, indeed, the default — way to mine. Beginning miners are steered toward mining pools; mining solo doesn't even register as an alternative.[183]

What *is* surprising, though, is the consolidation of power into the hands of just a few pools. The top pools are always jostling for position, and pools are always emerging or going out of business, but generally, we've found that the top 15 pools mine about 95%

of all Bitcoin blocks.[184] And, generally, the top 5 pools control between 60-75% of all Bitcoin mining.[185][186][187][188]

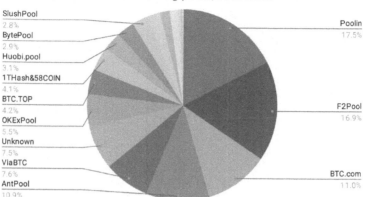

Market share of Bitcoin mining pools, Feb. 2020

At the time of writing, the top 4 mining pools control 56% of all hash power, meaning that they mine 56% of all blocks. Data source: Blockchain.com[189]

In some cases, some pools become so powerful that they control a majority or near-majority of the whole Bitcoin network's hash power. In 2014, the now-defunct pool GHash.io controlled 55% of all hash power,[190] and Bitmain's pools (BTC.com and AntPool) once owned 42% of all hash power.[191]

These cases were concerning not just because of the usual problems with monopolies but also because of the threat of a 51% attack. Remember that any person or entity who controls over half of all hash power could out-mine everyone else combined, which would let them create the new longest chain, which in turn would let them rewrite history and steal funds. Individuals can't ever hope to reach such power, but mining pools — as the GHash and Bitmain stories show — can reach that quite easily.

Now, Bitmain never reached the magic 51% (or, rather, 50% + 1 hash per second) benchmark, but GHash was above it for a few days.[192] To calm the community's nerves, the GHash CIO swore to never mount a 51% attack[193] and pledged to cap GHash's market share to 40% going forward.[194]

Bitcoin dodged a bullet that time, but ever since, Bitcoiners have remained afraid at the power mining pools hold over the future of the currency.

Chinese control

Another surprising feat of centralization is that most of the top pools are based in China; at the time of writing, Chinese pools control over 80% of the Bitcoin network's hash rate and thus mine 80% of the world's bitcoins,[195] a figure that's in line with historical estimates.[196]

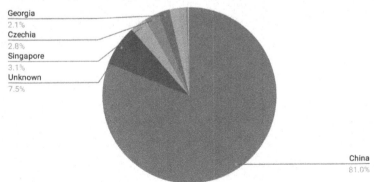

Countries' Bitcoin mining market share, Feb. 2020
Blocks mined by pools in each country

Georgia 2.1%
Czechia 2.8%
Singapore 3.1%
Unknown 7.5%
China 81.0%

Most of the top pools are Chinese: Poolin, F2Pool, BTC.com, AntPool, ViaBTC, BTC.TOP, 1Thash&58COIN,[197] OKExPool,[198] BytePool,[199] and WAYI.CN. Other countries' pools barely register.[200] Data source: Blockchain.com[201]

The largest non-Chinese pool, at the time of writing, is the Singaporean[202] Huobi.pool, which controls a grand total of 3% of Bitcoin's hash power.[203] (That pool's holding company, Huobi, was founded in China and still has close ties there. The largest unambiguously non-Chinese mining pool is the Czech SlushPool,[204] which controls just 2.8% of Bitcoin's hash power.[205])

And let's not forget that the Chinese company Bitmain owns 70-80% of the market for Bitcoin mining hardware.[206]

The problem here is that the Chinese government likes to exercise control over its top tech companies.[207] This means that the Chinese government could easily censor or interfere with the Bitcoin network, limit mining, or otherwise harm the Bitcoin ecosystem,[208] something it's threatened to do repeatedly.[209]

A powerful central government and a handful of big companies could control the future of Bitcoin. This is not the world that Satoshi envisioned.

Chapter 4.
Altcoins

While [cryptocurrencies] may pose risks related to law enforcement and supervisory matters, there are also areas in which they may hold long-term promise, particularly if the innovations promote a faster, more secure and more efficient payment system.
                    —Ben Bernanke, former Federal Reserve Chair[1]

BITCOIN ISN'T the only cryptocurrency in town. There are well over 2000 competing cryptocurrencies, known as *altcoins*,[2] each with its own features, mining algorithms, and (in some cases) blockchains. Some are specialized for particular kinds of payments, others aim to build a platform for apps, and others just seek to improve on Bitcoin's flaws. Altcoins have gotten bigger and bigger over time — Bitcoin controlled 90% of the cryptocurrency market back in 2015 but just over 60% at the time of writing.[3]

Bitcoin's forks

In 2016, the early Bitcoin developer and former Google engineer Mike Hearn called Bitcoin a failed experiment, citing many of its flaws:[4]

- Low capacity: about 3 transactions per second.
- Highly unpredictable fees and waiting times, especially in periods of high demand.
- Remarkable centralization in the hands of a few (mostly Chinese) miners, who in Hearn's view refuse to make changes that would make Bitcoin more popular because that would eat into their mining profits.
- The community's inability to agree on anything — including a popular amendment to grow the *block size*, or the number of transactions that can fit in a block. This would have let Bitcoin handle more payments per second, with fewer fees and lower waiting times.
- A "civil war" in the Bitcoin community over the block size increase amendment, which led to widespread censorship of opposing views on the official Bitcoin subreddit, forums, and website.

Hearn mused, "Would you care about a payments network that had [these flaws]? I'm going to hazard a guess that the answer is no."[5]

To show how centralized Bitcoin had become, Hearn shared a memorable story: this handful of men sitting on stage at a Bitcoin conference controlled 90% of the world's Bitcoin hash power.[6] Source: Jameson Lopp[7]

Bitcoin Cash

Hearn believed that these flaws couldn't be fixed due to the community's dysfunction and the chokehold that a powerful few held over the currency's future. So he decided to take the nuclear option and create a *hard fork* of Bitcoin in 2017, splitting the currency in two.[8]

Hard forking a cryptocurrency is like deciding that you didn't like the last three Harry Potter books and writing your own versions of them. Your Harry Potter series and J. K. Rowling's official series would share the same first four books, so they'd have the same backstory, main characters, and plot essentials. But after the fourth book, the two series would diverge, each introducing its own characters and storylines in the remaining three books.

When Hearn hard forked Bitcoin, he did something quite similar. His new cryptocurrency, called Bitcoin Cash, shared Bitcoin's pre-2017 blockchain, so all past Bitcoin transactions — including Satoshi's genesis block and Hanyecz's pizza purchase — were also part of Bitcoin Cash's official history. But all Bitcoin blocks mined after the split wouldn't be part of the Bitcoin Cash blockchain, and all Bitcoin Cash blocks mined after the split wouldn't be part of the main Bitcoin blockchain.[9]

Due to Hearn's frustration over Bitcoin's inability to scale, Bitcoin Cash increased the block size eightfold, with an option to increase it further over time. As a result, Bitcoin Cash's larger blocks would be rejected by the main Bitcoin software, while Bitcoin Cash would reject the smaller Bitcoin blocks, making the two blockchains incompatible.[10] (Backward-incompatible changes like these are known as *hard forks*, while backward-compatible changes are known as *soft forks*.[11])

Many of the key parts of Bitcoin stayed the same in Bitcoin Cash, though. For instance, both currencies have slowly-decreasing block rewards[12] that will result in no more than 21 million coins ever being mined.[13] Hearn preserved the features that he thought were useful and threw out the ones he didn't like; this flexibility makes hard forks attractive to crypto-leaders with strong opinions.

As soon as the split happened, all Bitcoin users had an equal number of bitcoins (known in shorthand as BTC) and Bitcoin Cash coins (known as BCH). Anyone whose wallet software supported Bitcoin Cash could thus double their coins for free,[14] although (perhaps as a result of this) each BCH has only ever been worth between 0.03 and 0.25 BTC.[15]

Thus, the outcome of Bitcoin's "civil war" was a breakup of Bitcoin, with the people hungry for change going to BCH and those who preferred the status quo sticking with BTC. Bitcoin and Bitcoin Cash's blockchains, software, community, developers, and roadmap are all different now.

Who "won"? You could say that BCH won because it won "independence" and peeled off some Bitcoin backers. But BCH's *market cap*[a] — the total value of all coins in circulation, and a popular metric of a cryptocurrency's success — is just 5% of BTC's at the time of writing.[16]

Forks on forks

Interestingly, in 2018 Bitcoin Cash itself was hard forked. A small band of developers, led by the controversial figure Craig Wright (who claims he is Satoshi[b]), hard forked Bitcoin Cash to create Bitcoin SV (for "Satoshi's Vision"). Wright argued that Bitcoin Cash was too much of a deviation from Satoshi's original vision for Bitcoin and hence made Bitcoin SV closer to the currency that Satoshi laid out in his seminal whitepaper announcing Bitcoin.[17]

Few miners defected from Bitcoin Cash (also known, somewhat confusingly, as Bitcoin ABC), and few exchanges started offering Bitcoin SV for sale.[18] Thus, Bitcoin SV was generally perceived as the loser of the mini-war,[19] but the beauty of the cryptocurrency world is that any currency, no matter how unpopular, can still exist.

---

[a] Short for *market capitalization*. The term is often used for stocks, too.

[b] You can read about Wright's claim in Appendix C.

The plot thickened further in February 2020, when Bitcoin SV was hard forked to implement an upgrade called Genesis, which purists said would make Bitcoin SV even closer to what Satoshi laid out in his paper. Fortunately for Bitcoin SV, almost all miners were on board with this upgrade, so nobody turned the old version of Bitcoin SV into a new currency.[20]

The takeaway is that the cryptocurrency space is chaotic, dynamic, and full of healthy competition. In our mind, "forkability" is one of the best features of cryptocurrencies and proof of the benefits of cryptocurrency development being done in the open, with code and debates happening in public.[21] Meanwhile, there's no way to spin off popular products like Amazon or Uber, keeping some parts of the code but throwing away features you don't like. You can't even see the code behind them.

Ethereum

The world's most famous altcoin, though, has little to do with Bitcoin or its associated civil wars. It's called Ethereum, and it views cryptocurrencies as more than simply payment tools or investment vehicles.

Ethereum was first described in a 2013 whitepaper[22] by the Russian-Canadian computer scientist Vitalik Buterin, then just 19 years old.[23] Buterin's big idea was that blockchains can do more than just record transactions: they can run code, host apps, store data, and really do any kind of computation.[24]

Vitalik Buterin, the inventor of Ethereum. Source: TechCrunch via Flickr[25]

Smart contracts

Ethereum thus adds the concept of *smart contracts*, or mini-apps that live on the blockchain, to cryptocurrency. Smart contracts can follow rules and move money, data, and other assets around accordingly.[26] They have addresses just like people do, and you can send them commands (with a small fee) to make them act.[27] In this way, they're a bit like vending machines on the blockchain: put money in, get a predictable item out.

Take gambling as an example. Imagine if many gamblers sent $20 in *ether* (the currency used in Ethereum, also known as ETH) to a smart contract's address the day before Super Bowl Sunday, along with a message saying which team they think would win. After the Super Bowl ended, the smart contract would check with ESPN to see which team won;[c] the gamblers that backed the winning team

---

[c] Yes, this gambling smart contract wouldn't cut out human institutions altogether. It would still have to check ESPN to get

would earn a certain amount of money, the losers would get nothing, and the smart contract would keep a few dollars for itself as profit for its creator.

Or imagine an insurance smart contract. An orange farmer in Florida might agree with an insurance agent that the agent would pay the farmer $1000 if there was a crop-destroying frost that winter, and the farmer would pay the agent $100 if not. The farmer would send $100 in ether to the contract, and the agent would send $1000.

Throughout the winter, the smart contract would check the Weather Channel's weather report. If it ever detected a temperature below 32°F, it would send all $1100 in its vault (minus, perhaps, a small fee) to the farmer. If the winter passed and there was never a sub-freezing temperature, the smart contract would send all $1100 (minus whatever fee) to the insurance agent.

There are plenty more ways you could use a smart contract: for auctions, voting, crowdfunding, and more.[28] The remarkable part of smart contracts like these is that they will always operate as intended — once they're set in motion, humans can't mess with their behavior. What's more, many smart contracts are made *open-source*, meaning that anyone can see the code they run.[29] Smart contracts, then, are like transparent vending machines: you know not only what you'll get out but also how the machine dispenses it.

If you use smart contracts, you don't have to trust any humans or institutions like the notoriously shady bookies[30] who take bets or often-greedy insurance companies with confusing policies.[31] This

---

sports scores. Non-blockchain-powered institutions that smart contracts have to trust, like ESPN in this example, are known as *oracles*.

takes Bitcoin's idea of "cutting out the middleman" one step further.[32]

More broadly, not having to trust companies or institutions could be liberating. Imagine if you find a great pair of shoes on an e-commerce website you've never heard of. You might feel hesitant paying the website because you can't be sure if the site will ever ship you the shoes. But imagine if that site ran on smart contracts: you'd put money into a pot, and the money would only get paid out to the store if FedEx or UPS reported that the package arrived at your house. You'd have no fear using that site — or any other new e-commerce site. (You'd still have to trust FedEx or UPS, so there's a hole in the decentralization, but it's better than trusting the questionable site.)

That's not to say that smart contracts are flawless. As one critic put it, they're neither *smart* nor *contracts*. That is to say, "smart" things can adapt to unexpected situations. Smart contracts, which run robotically and can only handle things written into their code, aren't adaptable.[33] What if the Super Bowl is, for whatever reason, postponed? What if there are credible allegations of cheating and Las Vegas decides to cancel all bets? Our smart contract couldn't handle these or all the other possible problems that might arise.

And "contracts" are legally binding; you can take someone to court if there's a dispute in the contract or if someone breaks it. But in our orange insurance case, what if the smart contract read the temperature as 31°F but the insurance company's data said the temperature was 33°F? In other words, what if the smart contract decided to pay out the claim but the insurer didn't want it to? There would be no way to resolve the dispute; the smart contract would just do whatever it had been programmed to do.[34]

So while smart contracts won't get rid of lawyers or courts (or, regrettably, even bookies), as many Ethereum backers might hope,[35] they are an interesting new model of computation, and they could have their uses in less legally- or monetarily-fraught applications.

DApps

You can bundle together smart contracts to make more sophisticated Ethereum-based apps, known as *decentralized apps*, or *DApps* (rhymes with "maps").[36]

Imagine if you made a DApp version of YouTube. You could have a smart contract that collected money from advertisers and auctioned off ad slots to the highest bidder, a smart contract that paid video creators based on viewership, a smart contract that flagged videos that violated copyrights, and so on.

Because this DApp would just be a bunch of autonomous smart contracts talking to each other, it would operate like clockwork, with no human intervention. Think of it as a giant vending machine. You could recreate most of the functionality of YouTube — but without the YouTube company. By cutting out YouTube, this DApp could remove the frequent policy changes that often confuse small-time creators and threaten to ruin their businesses.[37]

Similarly, you could make a decentralized app store with smart contracts to track reviews and ratings, let developers upload a new app, gather payment from an advertiser and put their app at the top of rankings, and let users pay developers for an app. This app store would also run autonomously. It would cut out the companies that usually run app stores, which often introduce new policies that are hostile to users and developers, such as when Apple banned certain adblockers from the App Store[38] or started taking a 30% cut of all in-app purchases, which many developers decried as unfair.[39]

Of course, cutting out the middleman isn't always a good thing. Platforms like YouTube, Facebook, Twitter, and others do good work[d] stopping fake news.[40][41] Amazon cracks down on price gouging and scammy products.[42] YouTube's thousands of human moderators block some truly awful content, like images of violence, cruelty, and child pornography, from getting on the platform.[43] And Apple, for all the complaints about how it handles the App Store, has blocked apps that promoted stalking[44] and youth vaping,[45] among others.

What's more, algorithms can be just as cruel as people; you'll know what we mean if you've ever encountered brutal surge pricing on Uber or Lyft. And, without people to watch them, algorithms can do some unfair things.

For instance, when there was a shooting in downtown Seattle in January 2020, public transit was shut down, and Uber and Lyft prices automatically started surging as people sought to flee the area.[46] There were reports of $100 Ubers to get out of downtown.[47] The companies were widely criticized for this practice,[48] and rightfully so, but they quickly refunded drivers who took overpriced rides.[49] If Uber or Lyft had been run as DApps, there would have been no way to right this wrong — and the cold logic of the algorithms would have kept marching on.

Just like with money, middlemen bring costs and benefits. It's not always a good thing to get rid of them, but with DApps, at least there's an alternative to middlemen for situations where getting rid of them makes sense.

---

[d] Some more than others, but at least they're trying.

The app ecosystem

Indeed, there are some interesting Ethereum-based DApps out there. Storj lets businesses pay users to store files on unused space on their laptop.[50] Golem lets scientists and artists crowdsource computing power from everyday people's laptops to crunch huge datasets, render computer graphics for movies, and so on.[51] Augur is a decentralized (i.e. bookie-free) prediction market, which lets people gamble on the outcomes of future events,[52] like the winners of upcoming elections or how much a country's GDP will grow this year.[53]

All the startups behind these DApps take a cut of the transactions happening on their platforms, but otherwise they don't (and, in many cases, can't) interfere with what's happening on the platform.[54] For the apps we mentioned, the activity is pretty harmless, so the lack of a middleman isn't a big problem.

CryptoKitties

We'd be remiss to ignore the first Ethereum DApp that made headlines, and perhaps the most popular DApp of all time: a virtual cat breeding game called CryptoKitties.[55]

On CryptoKitties, you can buy and sell cats with ether, and you can have two of your cats breed to produce a kitten that inherits some features from each parent.[56] CryptoKitties became incredibly popular in 2017; at one point, 15% of all Ethereum transactions were for CryptoKitties' smart contracts.[57] The game became so popular, in fact, that it clogged the Ethereum network, slowing down other payments.[58] At one point, 30,000 Ethereum transactions were stuck waiting to be processed because of CryptoKitties.[59]

CryptoKitties for sale. At the time of this screenshot, 0.01 ether was worth about $2.50, so these cats cost between $15 and $100 each. Source: Greg McMullen[60]

There's also a robust economy around CryptoKitties, and fans have written all manner of guides to explain how to optimize your breeding and make the most money.[61] (Apparently, the strategy is to get an original-generation cat and *hodl*,[62] as you might do with a vintage baseball card.) One cat sold for over $113,000,[63] leading the media to dub the fad "digital Beanie Babies."[64]

Genesis

Kitty #1 · Gen 0 · Fast Cooldown ⓘ

Stimpson J. Cat
Owner

Genesis, the first-ever CryptoKitty. It sold for $113,000 in 2017.[65] Source: CryptoKitties on Twitter[66]

As intricate as CryptoKitties' breeding algorithm and economy are, what's truly interesting is its model of ownership. In a normal game like Fortnite, the game's owner tracks which items you own on their servers. If that game ever shuts down, or if the owner decides to take away your belongings for some reason, all your virtual goods will be gone.[67]

But with CryptoKitties, your ownership is stored on the blockchain, so you will "own" the cat as long as the Ethereum blockchain stays alive (which is to say, as long as someone, somewhere is running the Ethereum software). The owners of CryptoKitties can't take your cats away from you, and, crucially, if someone were to fork CryptoKitties, you could import all your old cats into this new app. You can't do this with games today — you can't import your possessions into a Fortnite clone.

These properties led art critics to hail the blockchain as the potential future of arts and culture: there's finally a way to prove that you, and only you, own a piece of digital art.[68]

The DAO

Ethereum isn't all fun and cats, though; it's had its own share of controversy. This controversy centered around *The DAO* (it stands for *decentralized autonomous organization*[e]), a sort of decentralized venture capital fund launched in April 2016. Potential investors would send money (in the form of ether) to The DAO, and in exchange they'd get voting *tokens*.[69]

Ethereum tokens are virtual trinkets that any smart contract (or DApp) can make and hand out to users; users can trade tokens around and, in some cases, "redeem" them with the smart contract.[70] These voting tokens were a good example; the cats in CryptoKitties are also represented as tokens.[71] These tokens are implemented with the *ERC-20* technical standard, so they're commonly called *ERC-20 tokens*. [72]

Anyway, investors would use their voting tokens to vote on startups they wanted to invest in, and winning startups would automatically get a slice of the fundraising pie. It was a radically new model of venture capitalism: partners and hierarchy were out, and democratic decision-making was in.[73]

The DAO quickly became very successful, raking in $150 million from 11,000 investors in 28 days.[74] But the smart contracts behind The DAO were filled with bugs and security holes, and in June

---

[e] "DAO" is a generic term for any decentralized company or other organization. The DAO (always with the capitalized "The") was just the most famous DAO.

2016, an unknown hacker exploited an unknown bug[75] to steal 3.6 million ether, then worth about $50 million, from The DAO's coffers.[76] This was a massive amount of money: about 14% of all ether coins that had been mined up to that point.[77]

Ordinarily, it's a good thing that you can't alter past transactions tracked on a blockchain. But in this case it was crippling because there was no easy way to undo the hack of The DAO. The only way to undo the hack was to hard fork Ethereum and create a new blockchain, and thus a new currency, that undid the hack.[78]

This led to a massive philosophical debate between anti-fork and pro-fork activists. Anti-fork activists argued that "code is law," a common saying in crypto circles. In other words, the smart contract was programmed badly, but it did exactly what it was programmed to do. Even though we might not like what the smart contract did, it followed all the rules, so we shouldn't be claiming that it was wrong. Past transactions on the blockchain aren't meant to be changed. In short: we designed this system a certain way, and we shouldn't overturn it just because it had one outcome we didn't like.[79]

On the other side were pro-fork activists, who argued that the blockchain had to serve the people and not the other way around. They argued that the theft was unethical and that the Ethereum community had to roll it back to signal that such actions wouldn't be tolerated. Just as we can amend past laws when they no longer serve our needs, we should be able to amend Ethereum's rules when they lead to a bad outcome.[80]

In July 2016, the pro-fork activists were tired of the debate and decided to hard fork the Ethereum blockchain, creating a new version of the currency that returned stolen money to investors. This new version, confusingly, kept the original name Ethereum.

The anti-fork group continued to recognize the original, unaltered blockchain as the official one; this currency took the name Ethereum Classic.[81f]

While the debate was heated, at least there was a peaceful, constructive way to settle it. Again, the ability to hard fork blockchains was tremendously useful here.

Brave & BAT

Ethereum's ERC-20 tokens[g] are quite powerful. In fact, you can actually create a whole new cryptocurrency with these tokens: you just need a smart contract to hand out a limited number of tokens to users. Then, as long as there's someone willing to exchange your tokens for ether (or dollars) and vice versa, you have a scarce asset that can be traded around and can be converted to or from other forms of money. In other words, you have a currency![82]

These token-cryptocurrencies behave a lot like normal cryptocurrencies (which have their own blockchains), except tokens can't be mined; they're usually handed out by some other institution or algorithm.[83]

One of the best-known such token-cryptocurrencies is the *Basic Attention Token*, or BAT. BAT was created by Brendan Eich, the co-founder of Mozilla (the nonprofit behind the popular Firefox browser), in 2017. It goes hand-in-hand with the privacy-focused Brave web browser, which Eich had created in 2015.[84]

---

[f] The old Ethereum became Ethereum Classic; the hard-forked version adopted the Ethereum name.

[g] There are non-ERC-20 Ethereum tokens, but ERC-20 is so much more popular that "Ethereum token" equals "ERC-20 token" for almost all purposes.

Brave, the privacy-focused web browser that offers users free BAT (i.e. money) for watching ads. Source: Brave[85]

Eich created BAT because he was unhappy with the state of online advertising: nonstop ads eat up users' battery and mobile data, users are followed by an army of trackers as they browse, Google and Facebook own the vast majority of the market, and ad targeting technology is still poor. He blamed the middlemen — Google and Facebook's ad exchanges — for this unfortunate state of affairs.[86]

Eich's idea was to cut out the middlemen and have advertisers pay publishers (the sites that show ads, like the *New York Times*) and users directly with BATs. Because the mainstream web browsers don't support built-in cryptocurrency payments, Eich decided to build that functionality into Brave.[87]

The basis for payment is attention. Brave users are given BATs based on how much attention they pay to ads, and publishers are given BATs based on how much attention Brave users pay to ads on their platforms.[88] (Note that you can't mine BATs; you rely on Brave to give them to you.)

As you might expect by now, that payment system is built on smart contracts. When an advertiser creates an ad, it sends a few cents in BAT to a smart contract. When a Brave user views that ad, the smart contract is "unlocked" and the money within is paid out: some to the user, some to the publisher that hosted the ad, and some to Brave.[89] Eich and company argue that this system reduces fraud, improves the data given to advertisers and publishers, and protects user privacy better than the current advertising system.[90]

It remains to be seen whether BAT will achieve mass popularity, but its vision for a new business model for the web makes a lot of sense.

Currently, the incentives are all misaligned: advertisers are incentivized to make advertising as intrusive and annoying as possible, publishers are incentivized to cram ever-more ads on the page, and consumers are incentivized to install adblockers because they get nothing but misery from ads.

You only have to look at the absurd ad-blocking arms race to see how broken the system is: first there were adblockers, then websites started installing tools to hide web pages from people who were using adblockers,[91] and now there are add-ons for adblockers that stop websites from using that tactic.[92] First adblockers, then adblocker killers, then adblocker killer killers.[h]

But BAT seems able to align the incentives properly: everyone benefits when a user views an ad, and everyone loses when ads make a website experience bad. Under this theory, users won't want to install adblockers (who would pass up free money?), advertisers will make ads that people actually like,[i] and publishers

---

[h] We look forward to seeing websites start blocking anyone who uses these adblocker killer killers.

[i] Or, at least, don't hate.

won't make websites that are so ad-filled that users leave. It might just work.

Stablecoins

While Bitcoin aims to be an investment vehicle and Ethereum aims to be an app platform, another class of cryptocurrencies — *stablecoins* — aims to be just a classic payment system.

Seeking stability

As we saw earlier, the three main things that hold Bitcoin back from being a viable payment system are the fees, waiting times, and volatility. The first two can be fixed quite easily through various technical upgrades — remember SegWit and Lightning — or just by changing the rules around mining. Bitcoin Cash aimed to do this by increasing the block size. Another altcoin named Litecoin (LTC) offers very similar features to Bitcoin but with faster transactions (blocks take 2.5 minutes to mine instead of 10) and lower transaction fees (about 20 times lower, at the time of writing[93][94]). So fees and waiting times are solvable problems.

Bitcoin's volatility is the more fundamental problem:[95] there's a tradeoff between stability and growth, and as long as cryptocurrencies focus on growth, they won't have stability. And without stability, you'll have wild price fluctuations — remember how Bitcoin's price can jump[96] or crash[97] by 10% in a single day. With such fluctuations, people will be hesitant to pay with or get paid with these coins; you'd feel bad if you paid $100 for something but later realize you could have waited and had $110, and you'd feel worse if you earned $100 but saw 10% of its value vanish in a day.

Pegs

Meanwhile, stablecoins explicitly focus on, well, stability. These coins maintain a fixed exchange rate with fiat currencies like the dollar or euro.[98] The best-known stablecoin is called Tether: each Tether coin (known as a USDT, for US Dollar Tether) always trades at $1.[99] There are also Tether versions of yen, euros, and Chinese yuan.[100]

In economics terms, maintaining a fixed exchange rate like this is known as a *peg*. Many governments, seeking stability in their economies, peg their currencies to bigger, more established currencies, maintaining a constant exchange rate between their currency and the bigger one. For instance, 0.709 Jordanian dinars are always worth 1 US dollar, and 1.6 Nepali rupees are always worth 1 Indian rupee.[101]

Pegs are implemented by offering a simple trade: a central bank (or Tether) creates a *currency board*, a sort of bank counter that anyone can visit to exchange currencies at the predetermined rate.[102] Nepal, for instance, has a currency board that will let anyone buy or sell 1 Indian rupee for 1.6 Nepali rupees. In Tether's case, anyone can swap 1 USDT for $1 at any time.

Offering this trade ensures that the market's exchange rate stays fixed. If the market price of a USDT ever rose to $1.01, people would buy tons of USDT from Tether's currency board for $1 each and sell them on the market for a 1¢ profit per coin until the market price, depressed by all the selling, fell back to $1. And if the market price of a USDT ever fell to $0.99, people would buy tons of USDT from the market and sell it to Tether's currency board for a 1¢ profit per coin until the market price, driven up by all the demand, rose to $1.[103]

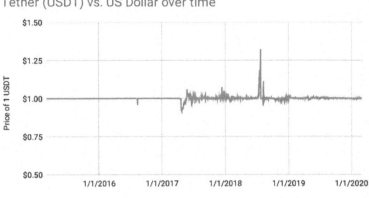

Save for a freak incident in 2018, Tether's price has been remarkably stable. Data source: CoinGecko[104]

The challenge with pegs is that the currency board offering the peg has to have enough of the bigger country's currency, known as the *reference currency*, sitting around. Nepal has to have a lot of Indian rupees in the bank to ensure people will always be able to exchange Nepali rupees for Indian rupees; if the bank ever runs out of Indian rupees, the peg will collapse. Similarly, Tether has to have enough US dollars in its coffers.

For many years, Tether committed to keeping $1 in reserve for every USDT in circulation.[105] With this approach, known as a *100% backed currency peg*,[106] Tether ensured that it could always honor its promised exchange rate — even if every single USDT holder tried to sell back all their coins for dollars. (The chances of that happening are very low, of course, but it would be devastating to USDT holders if the peg collapsed.)

Around 2018, analysts started suspecting that Tether wasn't really 100% currency-backed, meaning that the company might not really have owned $1 for every USDT in circulation.[107] (It was a tall task to begin with: there are 4.5 billion USDTs in circulation at the time of writing, so Tether would have to have $4.5 billion in the bank to be 100% currency-backed.[108]) That year, Tether tried to allay these fears by announcing that an outside law firm had confirmed that Tether was 100% dollar-backed.[109]

But in 2019, Tether admitted what many had long suspected: it wasn't 100% currency-backed. In March of that year, it quietly changed its website to say that USDTs were 100% backed by a mix of cash, cash equivalents (short-term, liquid bonds), and a vaguely-defined class of "reserves."[110] The company's lawyer said Tether had just 74% as many dollars and cash equivalents as USDTs in circulation[111] — meaning that the other 26% came from those murky "reserves."

Again, relying on "reserves" (which we imagine includes loans and stocks) doesn't in itself make Tether that much less stable. What rattled people was that Tether quietly went back on its word.

This points at a more fundamental problem with Tether: the stability of the currency is determined by the actions of a privately-held company — a middleman, so to speak. Without the Tether company, the Tether currencies would collapse. This runs counter to the spirit of blockchains and cryptocurrencies: the technologies should be able to run without human intervention, their future should be democratically decided, and they shouldn't rely on the trustworthiness of a small group of people.[112]

Dai

There is, however, a decentralized alternative to Tether: Dai, a stablecoin made by a group called MakerDAO.[113][j] Dai coins

---

[j] This is the same DAO acronym we saw in The DAO (an unrelated entity).

(technically, ERC-20 tokens[114]) are pegged at $1 a coin, but unlike Tether, MakerDAO doesn't hold any reserves or run its own currency board. Instead, MakerDAO has set up a clever economic system that automatically keeps Dai coins trading at around $1 a coin.[115]

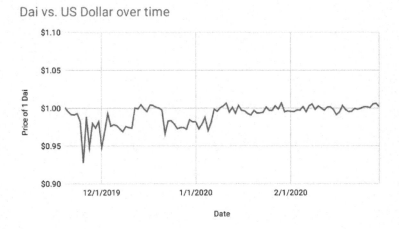

Dai[k] has been about as stable as Tether, but without the extreme spikes. Data source: CoinGecko[116]

You can get Dai coins by using a smart contract that creates a *collateralized debt position*, or *CDP*.[117] You send the smart contract some Ethereum coins (again, they're called ether) and can then borrow some Dai coins from it. To get your ether back, you return your coins plus a small interest fee to the smart contract.[118] In other words, you borrow Dai coins by using your ether as collateral; this loan is a CDP.

---

[k] This graph only considers the new version of Dai, known as the DAI coin. The old version of DAI, retired in 2019, is now known as SAI.

To keep the value of 1 Dai at $1, this system — known as the *target rate feedback mechanism* — reduces the amount of collateral you need when the price of a Dai goes too high and increases the amount you need when the price goes too low.[119] So if the price of a Dai grows to $1.05, people will create a bunch of Dais on the cheap, flooding the market with Dais, which will force the price back down. If the price of a Dai shrinks to $0.95, people will redeem their Dais to get their collateral back for a profit, shrinking the supply of Dais, which will force the price back up.[120]

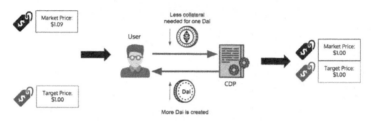

A diagram explaining Dai's target rate feedback mechanism, which aims to automatically stabilize the price of Dai. Source: Sid Shekhar[121]

So Dai's pegging system works a lot like a currency board: arbitrageurs make money if the exchange rate goes too high or low, but in doing so they push the exchange rate back to the pegged rate. But since the peg is maintained using smart contracts instead of a company, it's decentralized.

Dai coins are just one part of this system; MakerDAO runs another currency called **MKR**, which, like Dai, is implemented as an ERC-20 token.[122] MKR's value is free-floating (not stable), and you can only pay the interest fees on your loans (CDPs) with MKR.[123] So, in theory, the more people use Dai, the more demand there'll be for MKR, and the higher the price of MKR will go. Thus, investing in MKR means betting that Dai will grow in popularity.

Binance

Founded in 2017, the Chinese cryptocurrency exchange Binance has quickly become one of the most popular exchanges in the world,[124] supporting 1.2 billion transactions a day.[125] Its growth has been driven by a robust referral program that gives users a hefty commission on every trade made by people they invite to the platform, along with a tendency to offer niche but up-and-coming cryptocurrencies (voted on by users) for sale.[126]

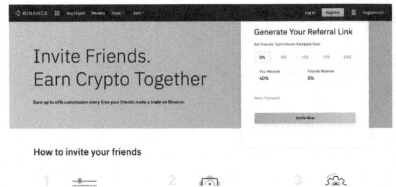

Binance's referral program, which offers users up to 40% commissions on all trades made by people they bring onto the platform. Source: Binance[127]

Binance also runs a coin called BNB;[128] Binance promotes the coin by giving you a discount on transaction fees if you pay with BNB.[129] Investing in BNB, then, is betting that Binance will grow in popularity. (Notice a trend here? Many crypto-startups offer cryptocurrencies whose values are tied, directly or indirectly, to the success of their products. They serve the same purpose as stocks do for regular companies: a way to raise money from investors and reward employees.)

The world is not enough

Binance isn't satisfied with running a massively popular cryptocurrency exchange. It also runs a sort of venture capital arm called Launchpad, which lets crypto-startups raise funds by selling their unique cryptocurrencies to Binance users; BNB is the only accepted form of payment.[130] These crypto-fundraising moments are known as *initial coin offerings*, or *ICOs*[131] — a crypto version of initial public offerings, or IPOs, when startups start selling shares on the stock market.

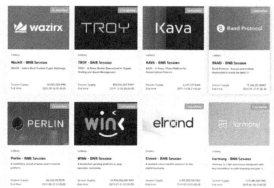

A few of the many crypto-startups seeking funding on Binance's Launchpad. These include a crypto exchange for India, a "cross-blockchain" finance platform, and a blockchain gambling platform. Source: Binance[132]

Binance also runs its own blockchain platform, called Binance Chain,[133] which lets crypto-startups create and issue their cryptocurrencies.[134] The Binance Chain is the basis for the Binance DEX, a decentralized cryptocurrency exchange (as opposed to Binance's regular, centralized exchange run by the Binance company[135]). Guess which popular cryptocurrency you can use to buy smaller cryptocurrencies on DEX? You got it: BNB.[136]

Binance also runs a charity arm that donates money to victims of natural disasters[137] and underfed children in Africa.[138] As you can guess by now, the money is donated in the form of BNB.[139]ᴵ

ᴵ You have to wonder if Binance pays its employees in BNB.

Binance has proven exceptionally skilled at building a crypto-ecosystem and using BNB to tie it all together. Small wonder, then, that BNB has — at the time of writing — the 9th-highest market cap of all cryptocurrencies.[140]

Monero

As we've mentioned, Bitcoin isn't really anonymous. Every single payment is stored publicly and permanently on the blockchain, so anyone can see how wealthy people are, who does business with whom, and where money has flowed.[141] If you can match a person to their address, you can see their entire payment history. In this way, it's worse for privacy than credit cards, because with credit cards at least your information is hidden from average people snooping around on the internet.

Average people may not be able to match you to your address, but the cryptocurrency exchanges you use sure can, and thus so can any government who can exert control over the exchanges. In 2017, the United States' Internal Revenue Service (IRS) forced Coinbase to hand over the names and Bitcoin addresses of people who had bought or sold large amounts of Bitcoin. Armed with this information, the IRS could identify and go after tax evaders.[142] (That's probably a good thing in this case, but it's alarming that governments could break the "anonymity" so easily — and you can imagine that a hostile government could crack down on civil liberties with this power.)

The Bitcoin ecosystem has created a few privacy safeguards, like encouraging people to use a new address for each transaction[143] and offering *Bitcoin tumblers*, which mix your coins with others' and hand back random coins, thus making it impossible to know where your coins came from.[144] Still, these are optional quick fixes, and privacy isn't baked into Bitcoin's design, leading critics to call these efforts "a Band-Aid over a stab wound."[145]

A privacy coin

Enter Monero, an altcoin that seeks to be private and anonymous to the core. Monero, which is popularly known as a *privacy coin*, uses a technology called CryptoNote to obscure the identities of the sender and receiver of every transaction.[146]

CryptoNote achieves this with two main techniques. First, multiple people are listed as potential senders for each transaction. This technique, known as *ring signatures*, obscures the true sender's identity. Second, recipients' identities are obscured by using *stealth addresses*: every recipient automatically gets a one-time address for each transaction, and only the person with that stealth address can see that the transaction happened in the first place.[147]

So, while all Monero payments are indeed stored on a blockchain, there's no way for the public to see who the sender or recipient of any transaction was. There's also no way to link transactions, so if you send money to someone, you'll have no idea if or when they spend that money.[148] (Both these things are possible with Bitcoin.)

Of course, the total anonymity comes with its downsides — it helps criminals evade scrutiny even more effectively than before.[149] It should come as no surprise that ransomware distributors have started asking their victims to pay in Monero rather than Bitcoin,[150] and hackers who seize control of supercomputers often prefer to use these machines to mine Monero instead of Bitcoin.[151]

Cryptojacking

Perhaps the most famous, and insidious, use of Monero is in *in-browser mining*. You can have your web browser run a snippet of

JavaScript code — the same kind of code that makes websites like Spotify and Google Docs interactive — to mine Monero coins.[152]

This is possible because Monero's mining algorithm is *ASIC-resistant*. While Bitcoin's mining algorithm only cares about how many trillion hashes a mining rig can do per second, Monero's algorithm requires computers to use a lot of memory (RAM) while mining. The idea is that ASICs are good at running a simple computation over and over, they lack the RAM that everyday computers use for running multiple apps, tabs, and games at once.[153]

Thus, a normal computer with a decent CPU and GPU should be able to mine Monero well enough, and ASICs should actually perform quite badly.[154] (This is a fragile system — mining companies once invented ASICs that cracked Monero's mining algorithm, forcing Monero to make emergency tweaks to its algorithm, thus setting off an arms race — but at least Monero is more ASIC-resistant than Bitcoin.[155])

A powerful gaming computer powered by Nvidia's GeForce GTX GPUs. These computers would struggle to mine Bitcoin, but they're quite good at mining ASIC-resistant cryptocurrencies like Monero.[156] Source: Wikimedia[157]

And because Monero's mining algorithm is so easy to run on a normal computer, even a web browser can mine for Monero coins, known as XMR. So, in 2017, a startup named CoinHive started letting website owners embed a small snippet of Monero mining code (written in JavaScript) on their websites. Visitors' browsers mine XMR, which flow to the website owner.[158]

This is an interesting idea in theory: website owners can now profit from their websites without having to rely on annoying and intrusive ads.[159] Games can also find a new revenue source by offering virtual goods, like extra lives or gold pieces, to users who let their browser mine for a few minutes.

The problem was that CoinHive wasn't used to create inventive new business models for the web. Instead, it was co-opted by shadier characters seeking to unethically make a buck. In 2017, the popular *torrenting*, or digital piracy, website The Pirate Bay started running CoinHive on visitors' browsers without letting them know or giving them anything in return.[160] This wasn't a harmless trick, either, since all that mining activity heats up visitors' computers, makes their fans kick into high gear, and drains their batteries.[161]

This tactic of hijacking a visitors' browser into mining coins for a shady operator is known as *cryptojacking*, and it's rapidly become a scourge across the internet.[162] It's incredibly lucrative, too: by one estimate, a website operator can earn over $300,000 a month by cryptojacking their visitors.[163]

Hackers have taken advantage of cryptojacking as well. In 2017, attackers hacked the popular Showtime website and quietly installed a cryptojacker,[164] thus earning the attackers XMR for each of Showtime's millions of visitors. Hackers mounted a similar attack on the LA Times' website in 2018.[165] Hacks became so widespread that cybersecurity analysts started calling cryptojacking the top malware threat they were tracking.[166]

You can see why cryptojackers love Monero: it's easy to mine it on a browser, and since it's totally anonymous, the crooks don't leave any fingerprints behind. This illustrates one of the fundamental tensions of cryptocurrencies: anything designed to promote privacy and anonymity — which are usually good things — ends up helping criminals more than anyone else.

Chapter 5.

Public Blockchains

The blockchain… is the biggest innovation in computer science—the idea of a distributed database where trust is established through mass collaboration and clever code rather than through a powerful institution that does the authentication and the settlement.

—Don Tapscott, author of *The Blockchain Revolution*[1]

After years of tireless effort and billions of dollars invested, nobody has actually come up with a use for the blockchain—besides currency speculation and illegal transactions.

—Kai Stinchcombe, co-founder of True Link Financial[2]

NOW THAT we've taken a deep dive into the world of cryptocurrencies, it's time to turn our focus to blockchains. Specifically, we'll start by looking at *public blockchains*, which are platforms where anyone can build apps for the masses to use. (We'll explore the opposite — *private blockchains*, which are used for company- or organization-internal purposes — in the next chapter.) It's still early days for public blockchains, but apps built with them have already seen some noteworthy wins and losses.

Online voting

It's no secret that voting machines are easy to hack.[3] Professionals can break into most voting machines in minutes by exploiting their numerous security flaws; hackers can then turn machines on and off, view votes, and change votes at will.[4] What's more, many US states' voting machines don't even keep a paper record of votes cast, so there's no way of knowing if a machine was compromised.[5]

Quite often, voting machines also fail to tabulate votes correctly. In 2000, a voting machine in Florida's Volusia County "gave" one candidate -16,000 votes.[6] (That's right, negative votes.) Many authoritative regimes have been accused of stuffing ballots or undercounting votes for their opponents[7] as well.

Voting also seems stuck in the past; if you can do everything from stock trading to shopping online, why do you have to trudge to a polling place and wait in line for hours to cast a vote? Estonia has made online voting work,[8] but it hasn't caught on everywhere because online voting is so easy to hack.[9] In one online voting experiment run in Washington, DC, a group of researchers managed to take full control over the online voting software, change all the votes, *and* make the confirmation page play the University of Michigan's fight song — all within 48 hours.[10]

Ideally, we'd have a voting system that keeps a rigorous, transparent count of how many votes each candidate got; is impossible to tamper with; and works online. If that sounds to you like something the blockchain could offer, you're right.

Blockchain and elections

Thus, many startups and researchers have explored the idea of putting elections on the blockchain.[11] Let's unpack what that means.

The idea of blockchain voting relies on *tokens*, which are digital assets whose movement can be tracked on the blockchain. On Ethereum, the most popular public blockchain platform, any app can issue tokens to users, and these users can send tokens to others the same way they might send ether (which, again, is the Ethereum cryptocurrency).

Anything of value can be represented as a token — for instance, a gold-exchange DApp could give you a gold token if you gave it an ounce of gold, you could trade around this token, and anyone could go back to the DApp to redeem their token for an ounce of gold.[12] (The big difference between tokens and ether is that anyone can create a token out of nothing and issue as many tokens as they want, whereas ether is the only official form of money on Ethereum, and new ether can only be made by mining.[13])

In blockchain voting, the government would issue a voting token to everyone eligible to vote in the election. Each voter could send their token to an address representing the person they wanted to vote for. Each "payment" of a voting token represents a vote and is stored on the blockchain. So because all votes are stored publicly on the blockchain, there's a robust paper trail, and anyone can count the votes to verify who won, removing the potential for error and corruption in vote tallying.[14]

The additional benefits of blockchains play a role here as well. Because blockchains are near tamper-proof,[15] hacking the blockchain to add or remove votes is nearly impossible. Because blockchains are so resilient — they survive as long as at least one computer has a copy of them — there's very little risk of the ledger of votes getting lost. And because the blockchain is decentralized, the government can't delete electoral results it doesn't like.

Challenges

The main challenge for blockchain voting is deciding who should get a voting token in the first place. This would probably involve people proving their identity online, but this is fraught with danger: Social Security numbers, which are the *de facto* unique identifiers for Americans, are disturbingly easy to guess if you know someone's birth date.[16] Lists of registered voters are also easy for adversaries to hack.[17] Plus, you'd have to rely on the government to decide who's allowed to vote, which goes against the goal of decentralization and would allow corrupt governments to still sway the election.

Estonia has managed to solve the verification problem by giving citizens electronic ID cards or mobile IDs tied to their smartphone; Estonians can enter these ID numbers into a website to prove who they are. A full 94% of Estonians have these secure digital IDs, making online voting possible.[18] While this approach works great in Estonia, a compact country of under 1.5 million people, it may not work as well in larger countries due to the difficulty of getting all residents IDs.

Another big problem is maintaining anonymity. Since all votes are stored publicly on the blockchain, anyone can see which Ethereum address voted for which candidate. And since the government has to choose which addresses get voting tokens, it probably would have to match real-world identities to addresses. This means the government, and possibly hackers, could figure out which voter owns which address and thus which candidate each voter chose.[19]

One potential solution to the anonymity problem is called *homomorphic encryption*,[a] which lets you encrypt each person's vote (so you can't know who any one person voted for) but still count the votes and figure out who won.[20]

Adoption

Blockchain voting has potential, but for now it's still in exploratory phases. Despite being the first country to allow online voting, Estonia still doesn't use the blockchain for voting.[21] The city of Zug, Switzerland[22] and the country of Colombia[23] have run successful pilots of blockchain-based voting, but it's still unclear whether these projects will see more widespread traction.

An immortal internet

In the late 1990s, GeoCities was the third-most visited website in the world.[24] It let anyone create websites for free, and at its peak there were millions of websites about Pokémon, bands, family vacation photos, and countless other topics.[25] Yahoo bought GeoCities for a then unheard-of $4 billion in 1999.[26] But in 2009, facing mounting financial troubles, Yahoo shut down the site, threatening to destroy millions of hours of human work and creativity.[27] GeoCities sites were only saved by the Herculean efforts of volunteers, who scraped all 900GB of site data shortly before all sites were taken offline.[28]

---

[a] The implementation of homomorphic encryption is beyond the scope of this book — it's something you'd study in college CS classes — but you can read about it in the endnotes referenced in this paragraph.

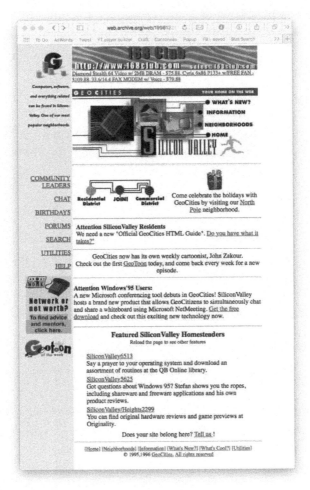

An example site that ran on GeoCities. Source: Ged Carroll via Flickr[29]

MySpace wasn't so lucky. The social network, which was the world's most popular in the early 2000s, lost 12 years' worth of user-uploaded music, photos, and videos due to a glitch in 2019.[30] MySpace had been the launchpad for many bands — but any music they'd put on MySpace and hadn't backed up was gone forever.[31]

Slow, fragile, forgetful

More generally, you can't rely on anything you see on the internet to still be around in a few years. One study found that web links have a half-life of just seven years: if you put a link to a webpage in a book or document or other webpage, there's a 50% chance that the link will no longer work after seven years (that is, it won't take you to the intended page anymore).[32] You can comfortably cite a Homer's *Odyssey*, which was written over 2000 years ago,[33] knowing that people will always be able to find the book you're referring to. But hoping a web link stays alive for just ten years is a risky bet.

There are services like the Internet Archive that, well, archive past versions of webpages, but their coverage is spotty and can't possibly capture every single webpage ever made. This problem of *link rot* is too pervasive.[34]

In fact, the problem is structural. Whenever your browser loads a webpage, like the *New York Times*' homepage, it asks a server for the latest copy of the page. The server is, more often than not, the only place where that content lives. If the server shuts down or deletes the page, you'll never be able to get that content again. This is a classic example of centralization, and web servers are a single point of failure.

The other problem with this centralization of content is speed. If you're in the US and visit a website whose nearest server is in Australia, reaching that server and getting the page back will take upwards of 300 milliseconds[35] — and at that point 80% of viewers can already notice lag.[36] To reduce this lag, you'd have to build servers across the globe, but this infrastructure can cost thousands or millions of dollars.[37]

As *TechCrunch* puts it, the internet — thanks in large part to its centralized model of webpages — is "slow, fragile, and forgetful."[38]

IPFS

A blockchain project known as the InterPlanetary File System, or IPFS, thinks it can change that. IPFS proposes a new model for the internet. In IPFS, webpages don't just live on a central server — anyone in the world can keep a copy of them.[39]

As an analogy, consider the ancient Library of Alexandria in Egypt, established in 334 BCE. It was long considered the world's capital of knowledge and learning,[40] containing over 40,000 scrolls of priceless information. But when the library burned in 48 BCE, those thousands of scrolls were destroyed — and since there were no backup copies of the scrolls, the knowledge on those scrolls was lost forever.[41] Had the Library of Alexandria let other libraries around the world store copies of the scrolls, the knowledge on those scrolls would have been much more likely to survive to the present day. IPFS views the current internet as the Library of Alexandria — too much information is kept in centralized places — and aims to spread information across multiple "libraries."

All IPFS users have a folder on their computer where they can store files or webpages. Unique fingerprints of these files, known as *hashes*, are stored on a blockchain. Anyone who wants a file just needs to look in the blockchain to see who has the file with that hash. Once they find the right person, they can copy the file from that person's IPFS folder. The trick is that, if you get a file from someone else's computer, you store a copy on your computer as well. Even if the original file is deleted, the copies stay.

This means that the most popular files and webpages will be backed up in hundreds of thousands of computers around the world, making them immune to the link rot that afflicts today's internet. What's more, because files are spread around the world, it's likely that everyone will be able to find a file stored on a computer that's geographically close to them, which makes accessing it faster.[42]

Think of IPFS folders as a bunch of public Dropbox or Google Drive folders — anyone can find, download, and copy files from anyone else. IPFS's blockchain just serves as a directory, showing you who has copies of the file you're looking for.

Additionally, every time a file is changed, that change is tracked on the blockchain as well. Anyone with an old copy of the file keeps it, and the new version of the file can propagate through the network independently. This means that anyone can see old versions of a file (kind of like the "track changes" feature in a Word document), ensuring that content is really permanent. Even if someone changes a webpage (say, to delete some information they want to hide), the old versions will live on — which is not possible in today's internet, where you get only the latest versions of webpages from the server.[43]

Currently, IPFS runs its own mini-internet; anyone can sign up for IPFS and start storing files and accessing files from others on the network.[44] IPFS hopes to one day dislodge the current internet and install its "faster, safer, and more open" alternative.[45] (While we're excited about reducing link rot, we'll note that a censorship-proof, distributed file sharing system like this makes digital piracy even easier.)

Airbnb for your hard drive

One hitch is that people may not be incentivized to store strangers' files on their hard drives. To fix this, a project called FileCoin aims to pay people who store copies of IPFS files on their computers.

The idea is that anyone who wants to access a file in someone else's IPFS folder needs to pay them a filecoin. You earn filecoins by either hosting files yourself or buying them off the market. It encourages good citizenship — the more you access others' files, the more files you should host yourself — and lets people with extra storage space make some money by earning and selling filecoins. In this way, it's like Airbnb for your hard drive: you can make money by renting out your extra room.[46]

And when people are paid to store files, they'll store more of them. This is great for IPFS, because it works best when many people store copies of files.[47] (If only one person is storing a file, IPFS is no better than the current internet.)

Hooters rewards on the blockchain?

In 2018, a North Carolina company called Chanticleer, which owns several franchised restaurants including some Hooters, announced that it would be partnering with a blockchain company called Mobivity to launch a blockchain-based rewards program. Anyone who ate at a Chanticleer restaurant would get virtual coins — stored on a blockchain — that they could redeem for free meals at other Chanticleer-owned restaurants or gift to other customers. The CEO of Mobivity proudly announced, "Eating a burger is now a way to mine for cryptocoins!"[48] Chanticleer's stock price soared 41% after the announcement.[49]

If you ignore that the Mobivity CEO comically misunderstood what mining is, you have to ask yourself: is using the blockchain for Hooters rewards really worth it? Using the blockchain to fix the internet or reinvent democracy — sure. But burgers?

Overkill

Adding a blockchain to an app comes at a cost. If you're building on Ethereum, each transaction will cost about 5-10¢ in fees,[50] which adds up. And the blockchain itself hogs a lot of space: the Ethereum blockchain weighs over 200GB at the time of writing,[51] and its growth isn't slowing anytime soon. And, no matter what blockchain you use, blockchains are *slow*: a classic centralized database called MySQL can handle 60,000 times more transactions per second than Ethereum (which itself can handle five times as many as Bitcoin)![52]

So it only makes sense to use a blockchain if the blockchain's unique strong points are necessary. In our minds, the top selling points of blockchains are that they're decentralized, trustless, transparent, and tamper-proof. And Chanticleer's blockchain-based rewards system needs precisely none of these strong points:

o   Decentralization means that you don't need to rely on middlemen, which are single points of failure and bring along fees and restrictions. The problem in Chanticleer's case is that rewards points can only be accepted at Chanticleer's restaurants — so if Chanticleer goes out business, all your rewards points become meaningless. This system is centralized, with Chanticleer as the middleman. Blockchains can enable decentralization, but only if the system is allowed to become decentralized. Unless Chanticleer allows any restaurant, anywhere to accept the rewards points, the system will remain centralized and the blockchain will add no value.

o   Blockchains enable trustlessness: nobody has to trust anyone else for the system to work. With Bitcoin, for instance, you don't have to trust banks or governments to process payments; you only need to trust that the Bitcoin software will work as intended. But, blockchain or no blockchain, you have to trust that Chanticleer will honor your rewards points. If they don't, you'll be left with a bunch of useless tokens. This is the opposite of trustlessness — so Chanticleer's program doesn't use this feature of blockchains at all. (So much for the Mobivity CEO's proclamation that his program would "transform traditional consumer rewards into something that the consumer can control;"[53] you don't really control rewards points if you have to hope a restaurant will accept them.)

o   Because they make every past transaction public and unchangeable (or *immutable*), blockchains are exceptionally transparent. All illegal payments made with Bitcoin can (in theory) be found by anyone, which you'll recall was useful when the FBI wanted to take down the Silk Road. However, we don't think anyone cares to know if you redeemed points for chicken wings at Hooters on Saturday — the transparency that this solution provides would not be very valuable.

o   Finally, mechanisms like proof-of-work make blockchains basically tamper-proof, which is great for security. However, we don't think anyone wants to steal burger rewards points for North Carolina restaurants, so this benefit is wasted.

In short, using a blockchain for this rewards program is like using a $50 golf club to pound in a nail: sure, it works, but you aren't using any of the tool's special abilities and, as such, you're wasting money. You'd be better off using a cheaper tool more specialized to the simpler task at hand: a $10 hammer or a standard database. By a standard database, we mean something that's conceptually just a giant Excel spreadsheet: it's not decentralized, trustless, transparent, or tamper-proof, but it's very good at just storing information. Chanticleer could just track all rewards points in a standard database (like MySQL, which we mentioned earlier) and get better performance and lower costs.

But, of course, announcing they were using a giant Excel sheet would not have sent Chanticleer's stock price soaring 41%. Blockchains were total overkill for this program, but Chanticleer just wanted to cash in on the hype.

Trademarks on the blockchain

In 2016, a London-based group noticed that musicians were having trouble trademarking their band names,[54] leading to identically-named bands bickering over who had the name first.[55] So the group launched a startup called BandNameVault, which would let any band register their name on a blockchain for $15.[56]

When you created a band, you could register that you thought of your band's name in a transaction on a blockchain. If anyone ever tried to give their band the same name as yours, you could point to your transaction and show that you already registered it.

From a technical perspective, this is a clever solution: because the blockchain is linear and virtually tamper-proof, it's very easy to prove that one transaction happened before another, and you can have confidence that the order wasn't compromised. It also helps, of course, that every transaction on the blockchain is public, so anyone can check the order of registration themselves. This process is much faster and cheaper than filing an official trademark with, say, the US Patent and Trademark Office (USPTO).[57]

But the case for BandNameVault falls apart under closer scrutiny. You can register your band name on the blockchain until you're blue in the face, but that doesn't mean anything in court. You could sue a new band for using your band's name and point to the blockchain as proof, but the courts would not recognize this random startup's blockchain as evidence. (What's to prevent a sleazy band from making a fake blockchain that says that their name came first?) The only way you can actually enforce your claim to a band name is to trademark it through a government agency like the USPTO.

The BandNameVault founder admitted as much himself: "a successful trademark application does offer a full set of legal protections and licensing opportunities that our simple registration serve does not."[58]

Now, if the USPTO announced it was going to store trademark registrations on a public blockchain, that would be different. But when a random startup tries doing it, its solution has no teeth and offers little of value. Storing things on the blockchain often leads to big efficiency gains, but efficiency is far from the only thing that matters; it's more important that solutions integrate with existing power structures. Blockchains are great technological innovations, but they aren't enough to drive social change — you have to think hard about getting people and institutions to change their behavior. In this case, BandNameVault would have done well to get government trademark offices or courts on board with their software before releasing it.

Silver linings?

It's not too surprising that the UK publication *The Register* asked readers if BandNameVault was "the worst Blockchain idea you've ever heard".[59]

But, for all its flaws, BandNameVault project raises an interesting question: how can you prove when it happened? That is, how can you show that you knew something, said something, or did something at a certain time? These days, you can forge photos, audio, and even videos.[60] Tweets and webpages are easy to delete.

So the traditional ways of proving when things happened aren't bulletproof. Blockchains provide one of the few reliable ways to prove when something happened, thanks to their linear nature and tamper-proof-ness.

If you record something on a reputable blockchain, there is little doubt that you recorded it. This is quite an achievement. The challenge, as BandNameVault shows, is getting people to care that you recorded it at all.

Decentralizing websites

When you type a webpage address, like *google.com/maps*, into your browser's address bar, your browser doesn't actually know what to do with it. Instead, it consults a giant address book of sorts, called a *Domain Name Service (DNS)*, to turn the *domain name* (the base part of the address, like *google.com* for *google.com/maps*), into a series of numbers known as the *IP address*. Your browser then knows how to fetch webpages based on their IP addresses.[61]

You can compare this process to calling someone on your phone: your phone doesn't know how to call people by name (you can't just punch in "Bill Gates" and hope to get on the line with him), so it looks up their names in your contacts list to get their phone numbers, which it knows how to make sense of.

The problem here is that DNSes are quite centralized; usually, your *internet service provider (ISP)*, a company like Verizon or Comcast, provides the DNS for you. If your ISP decides to remove the entry that pairs a certain website's domain name with its IP address, you won't be able to visit that website at all.[62] Google offers a free DNS in case you don't like your ISP's DNS, but there's the list of possible DNSes is still quite small.

This centralization was thrown into stark relief when, in 2011, US lawmakers floated a bill called the Stop Online Piracy Act, or SOPA, which aimed to crack down on piracy by forcing all American ISPs to remove the DNS entries of offending websites. The websites would still exist, but it would be impossible for Americans to reach them.[63]

SOPA didn't pass, but internet activists became alarmed at how easy internet censorship had become. A country could just force its handful of ISPs to remove a certain website from their DNSes and thus ban anyone from seeing them. (This isn't theoretical, either; China's "Great Firewall" uses the same tactic to block disapproved websites.[64]) And it's all made possible by the centralization of DNSes; the ISPs are a single point of failure, and single points of failure make censorship easy.

Decentralized DNS

Troubled by DNS centralization, a team of blockchain enthusiasts created an altcoin called Namecoin.[65] Anyone could register their website's IP address into the Namecoin blockchain, which functioned as a sort of DNS. Anyone could run the Namecoin software on their computer and look up the IP address of any website registered there, no matter what their ISP tried to block.[66]

Since blockchains are decentralized and peer-to-peer, there's no single point of failure that a censorious government can attack. And because blockchains are so secure, governments can't try to erase entries from this decentralized DNS.

It's a good idea, but it suffered from the *chicken-and-egg problem.* Website owners wouldn't bother registering their websites with Namecoin unless they knew people would use Namecoin and thus visit their sites. And consumers wouldn't bother downloading Namecoin unless they knew the websites they cared about most were registered there. The fatal problem was that consumers just didn't care enough about censorship to go through the hassle of Namecoin, according to Michael Dean, an early Namecoin backer.[67] And thus, the decentralized DNS never took off.

Decentralized website registration

Later, Namecoin had a more ambitious idea: replacing the website registration process, which is also centralized. When you start a website, you need to buy the domain name from a company known as a *registrar*; each domain ending (*.com*, *.org*, *.de*, *.jp*, and so on) is managed by a different registrar. But each registrar is ultimately managed by a company called ICANN, which means that ICANN could, in theory, delete any website's domain name and thus take it offline.[68]

So Namecoin introduced *.bit*, a new decentralized domain name ending. Anyone could register a *.bit* website on Namecoin's blockchain, and anyone running the Namecoin software could visit any *.bit* website.[69]

The problem was that you couldn't visit a *.bit* website unless you were running Namecoin's software, meaning that the chicken-and-egg problem was now in full effect. Plus, the Namecoin software was tedious to set up and required extensive configuration[70] and setting up a website was needlessly complicated.[71]

Unsurprisingly, the *.bit* domain ending failed to take off. Michael Dean said that only about 30 real *.bit* domain names were ever created, and they were all *mirrors* of sites with "traditional" domain endings, showing the same webpages from a different domain name.[72] (So there was no new content available on the Namecoin sites.) And just 5000 people had set up the software to view *.bit* sites.[73]

Meanwhile, because registering a *.bit* website was so cheap, it was flooded with hundreds of thousands of *squatted* websites,[74] or placeholder sites that took a popular name in the hopes of being sold for a profit later. Imagine buying, say, *facebook.bit* or *disney.bit* for $5 and selling it for $5 million if *.bit* took off. Suffice it to say that *.bit* was mostly used for shady purposes.

The final nail in the coffin for Namecoin was the team's poor cohesion and strategy. At one point they tried to partner with ICANN and Google, the same companies they were trying to "disrupt" — Dean called it "making a technology to circumvent governments and then handing it over to governments."[75]

The verdict is that Namecoin failed. NMC, the cryptocurrency you use to buy and sell domain names and DNS entries, isn't even in the top 200 cryptocurrencies by market cap, or the total value of all coins in circulation.[76] And, as Dean mentioned, usage of the products themselves is low.

The main reason Namecoin failed is that it underestimated people's inertia. Their solution may have been more decentralized and technologically sound than the current system, but setting up this kind of *two-sided market* (with consumers on one side and website makers on the other) was tremendously difficult, especially when *.bit* was so hard to use.

There's little evidence that Namecoin thought hard about these people problems; it seems they just focused on building a cool, technologically stronger product without thinking about how to actually get people to use it. As we've seen throughout this chapter, that's a common problem for blockchain apps: focusing too much on the technical problems without thinking about the people problems.

Chapter 6.

Business on the Blockchain

Anything that you can conceive of as a supply chain, blockchain can vastly improve its efficiency — it doesn't matter if it's people, numbers, data, money.

—Ginni Rometty, CEO of IBM[1]

P EOPLE BUILDING public blockchains have been thinking big: rearchitecting democracy, eliminating censorship, or modernizing trademarks. But there's another kind of blockchain to consider: a *private blockchain*. Instead of trying to create ambitious new services for everybody, private blockchains just try to automate and improve complex, inefficient, and largely manual systems inside enterprises.

Walmart and preventing foodborne illnesses

In 2018, reports of *E. coli*-tainted romaine lettuce shocked the United States, with over 200 people falling sick and 5 dying. It was "the most extensive and deadly [outbreak] to ever hit the produce industry."[2]

The problem was that nobody who got tainted lettuce could track it back to the source farm because the entire supply chain of produce — from the farm that grew it all the way to the supermarket that sold it — was so opaque and inefficient. The whole system was paper-based, and each company involved in the process only needs to be able to trace products "one step back and one step forward," meaning that tracing something multiple steps back involves talking to several independent companies.[3]

Tracking down where a piece of produce came from can take over a week — and, as a result, it took over 3 months for authorities to trace the tainted lettuce back to farms using water from a single canal in Yuma, Arizona.[4] Even after the source had been identified, nobody could really be sure if the lettuce they had gotten was tainted because it was so hard to trace the lettuce all the way back to the source.[5]

Shortly thereafter, Walmart announced it would be reforming its supply chain by requiring every company that sells them leafy greens to start putting their supply chain on a blockchain.[6] Each company would log each movement of products on a Walmart-owned blockchain, which Walmart had co-developed with IBM.[7] Each movement would be entered as a transaction on this blockchain, which is known as IBM Food Trust. Each transaction would encode *metadata* like the products' lot number, the time and date, and the products' origin and destination.[8]

How it works

Walmart could have built this solution on a public blockchain, such as by making an Ethereum DApp. But this comes with many costs: anyone can see your transactions (though you can encrypt the data in transactions to keep them private), you have to pay about 5-10¢ in fees for each transaction,[9] and you don't get to set the blockchain's rules or decide who gets to mine. These are deal-breakers for enterprises hoping to put entire business systems into a totally new system; the risks and costs are just too high.

Instead, private blockchains like the IBM Food Trust are custom-built blockchains that only store Walmart's supply chain transactions and that can only be viewed by select people.[10] Because Walmart and IBM own this private blockchain, they don't need to get third-party miners[11] and set fine-grained *access control* or *permissioning*, determining exactly which pieces of information each person can access at which times.[12]

At the same time, private blockchains maintain a lot of the benefits of public blockchains, such as decentralization (many computers still keep copies of the blockchain), immutability (proof-of-work still makes it hard for an attacker to forge blocks), and transparency (everyone can get exactly the information they need without having to hunt down people across companies).[13]

The results

The efficiency gains of Walmart's new leafy green supply chain were staggering. The supply chain process was now digitized, data was stored in a standardized format (the common blockchain could enforce a certain structure to the data), and everything was in one place. Walmart could now trace a given produce shipment to a Walmart all the way back to the original farm in 2.2 seconds,[14] an over one hundred thousand-fold speedup. What's more, Walmart could know exactly who was involved and where they were at each step.[15] This could help Walmart instantly identify and yank tainted food from shelves, and it could help authorities more quickly find and shut down farms making the tainted food. This solution could also identify where the supply chain gets slowed down and where food gets wasted.[16]

In short, this solution presented a powerful way to stop foodborne illnesses, food waste, and supply chain inefficiencies. And it was a hit: Walmart's VP of Food Safety announced shortly thereafter that *all* of Walmart's fresh fruit and vegetable suppliers, not just leafy green suppliers, would be required to track their supply chain on IBM Food Trust.[17] (It's estimated that 90% of all blockchain trials never turn into reality, so this program's success is rare.[18])

So, why the blockchain? Why couldn't Walmart just require suppliers to put supply chain information in a giant database or Excel sheet? We argued last chapter that the Hooters franchiser, Chanticleer, wasn't using blockchain's strengths and could have gotten away with a standard database, but in this case, Walmart was using blockchain's strengths effectively:

o The blockchain's decentralization is extremely helpful when enterprises need to keep data safe. If Walmart kept all its supply chain data in a single database stored on a single computer, it would be a ripe target for hackers and purveyors of *ransomware*, who encrypt a valuable file and threaten to throw away the key (thus making the file's contents permanently useless) unless they are paid.[19] A single, centralized source of truth is also vulnerable to natural disasters, power outages, and all manner of other misfortunes. Because many different parties keep their own copies of the blockchain, the blockchain is far less prone to these security problems.

o The blockchain's transparency is great for internal and external audits. Any eligible person can instantly see the path food took from farm to plate, whereas before they might need to hunt down many companies and ask each one to open their books. Because of the *access control* of private blockchains, select pieces of data could be opened to external auditors like the US's FDA or even the general public while keeping other data private.

o The blockchain's tamper-proof-ness is vital for something as important as a supply chain. A hack, or getting something wrong, could risk customers' lives and millions of Walmart's dollars.

o As we mentioned before, keeping everything in a single blockchain forces all data to be in the same standardized format, making it much easier to work with than data spread across multiple databases.

Note that none of these benefits are specific to food; any supply chain can benefit from the efficiency, security, speed, and transparency that blockchains offer.[20] We think supply chains are one of the *killer apps* of blockchain — a use case where a blockchain is head and shoulders above every alternative.

Stocks and blocks

If you want to sell an old book or buy a rare baseball card, you probably don't turn to your friends — it's pretty unlikely that anyone you personally know will want to buy or sell those things at exactly the price you're thinking. Instead, you're more likely to turn to a site like Amazon or eBay, which can efficiently match you to the small group of people around the world who want to buy that book or sell that card.

Something similar happens with stocks, futures, or other financial instruments. Whenever you buy or sell a stock, your shares appear and disappear instantly, as if by magic. But the odds of you personally knowing someone who wants to buy your shares of General Mills or sell you UPS shares are low.

So, instead, your broker or stock trading website turns to third parties known as *clearinghouses*, which are the eBays of stock trading: they match millions of sellers and buyers to each other so people can quickly and efficiently find trading partners.[21] If you're looking to sell 100 shares of a particular stock for $5000 and someone across the world wants to buy 100 shares for $5000, the clearinghouse will pair you up.

Clearinghouses also take on the risk of the transaction; they make sure the transaction goes through even if one side fails. If you sell 100 shares of stock for $5000 but the randomly-chosen buyer defaults, you'll still get your $5000, thanks to the clearinghouse.[22] Clearinghouses also make sure buyers and sellers are fiscally sound, take care of legal paperwork, and send data to buyers and sellers.[23] Overall, clearinghouses take care of all the dirty work and risk so that anyone can buy and sell stocks with a click, knowing that everything will work out seamlessly.

Clearinghouses are middlemen — they stand between buyers and sellers, for good reason — so, to increase efficiency and reduce costs, stock markets often employ software-based clearinghouses, known as *automated clearinghouses* (ACHs).[24]

By 2017, the Australian Stock Exchange (ASX)'s ACH software was aging, it decided to give the blockchain a go.[25] This is a natural pairing because clearinghouses work similarly to smart contracts: they take money from the buyer and stocks from the seller, run some checks, and swap the assets once both sides were verified.[26] If you turned all the complex logic of a normal ACH into a smart contract, you could score big wins in efficiency and transparency.

The details of the ASX's blockchain-based ACH weren't made public, but we assume their implementation is similar to what we have just outlined. All money and stocks are represented as tokens, and all stock sales are represented as blockchain transactions. All transactions are mediated by a smart contract, which takes in money tokens from the buyer and stock tokens from the seller, runs some checks, then swaps them.[27]

The benefits of smart contracts are large here. Smart contracts are predictable — like machines, they run pretty much the exact same each time — and all their actions are reliably stored on a blockchain. Meanwhile, the ASX's old solution was relatively messy (non-blockchain apps can get away with being laxer with precision and tracking), fragile, and slow. One market strategist predicted that this blockchain solution could, for these reasons, save ASX tens of millions of dollars from reduced fees, increased transparency, and lower bureaucratic complexity.[28]

The ASX isn't alone in having these needs. There are tons of stock exchanges and clearinghouses around the world, and many could benefit from blockchains just as ASX did. One report found that the stock exchange industry could save $20 billion from blockchain-based clearing.[29] And that's just stock exchange clearinghouses; other financial markets (especially futures markets) rely heavily on clearinghouses as well.[30]

But the ASX's blockchain adoption had some hitches. The technology was so new that the ASX's solution took two years to develop,[31] and even then the launch got delayed by six months.[32] This is the cost of being on the cutting edge; that might be too much for some financial institutions (usually a risk-averse bunch) to stomach.

Another issue is that the law hasn't had time to catch up with blockchains, which is problematic for heavily-regulated industries like finance.[33] Current financial laws and regulations don't have any concept of crypto-tokens, distributed ledgers, and smart contracts, and the ways these tools operate often clash with the laws and regulations currently on the books. For instance, courts can throw out contracts that they deem "unconscionable," which are when one party has so much more bargaining or financial power that the contract just isn't fair.[34] But smart contracts execute automatically; you physically cannot alter or void them once they are set into motion (indeed, that's part of the appeal). So laws need to be changed to find new ways to stop unfair smart contracts, and on the flip side, anyone who starts using smart contracts instead of regular old contracts needs to find ways to keep their smart contracts in compliance.

In short, blockchains and smart contracts can lead to tremendous efficiency gains for the back offices of financial institutions like stock exchanges. But it's not as easy as dropping in a new piece of software: hot new tools like these come with growing pains and potential legal difficulties.

Xbox and game royalties

If you're publishing an Xbox game, you'll probably need to work with a small army of external contractors: musicians, special effects studios, character designers, and so on. And you'll need to ink complex royalty contracts with each of these contractors, setting rules, like, "we will pay the musician X% of all revenue after the first $Y million in sales, provided the game earns at least Z stars on this review site."[35] A typical game could have hundreds of contracts like these, and even simple contracts have several pages of criteria and formulas.[36]

Managing the complex terms of these contracts is a logistical nightmare, requiring huge teams of accountants to fax around reams of paper, sift through piles of Excel spreadsheets, and wade through endless emails.[37] And if the expected payment doesn't match the actual payment, accountants have to go through the time-intensive and error-prone process of *reconciliation*, where they need to hunt down every single piece of paperwork involved, read through all documents, and pick out and fix discrepancies.[38] For Xbox publishers, it could take up to 45 days for all royalties to be settled[39] — an unthinkably slow pace for the fast-moving gaming world.

Here's another way to look at the problem: royalty payments required accountants to manually compute royalties based on complex rules, and all the data needed to make those computations was scattered across many different data sources. Xbox wanted to automate royalty computations and bring all data into one place. So Xbox decided to build a blockchain-based royalty settlement system.[40]

Xbox turned all the complex royalty contracts into smart contracts, turning all the complex legalese into precise mathematical formulas. That example rule we showed earlier —

"we will pay the musician X% of all revenue after the first \$Y million in sales, provided the game earns at least Z stars on this review site" — would be turned into a smart contract that would compute the proper royalty based on input data like sales and ratings.[41]

Automated smart contracts are far more efficient than accountants reading through paper contracts, so they can compute royalties in seconds. And because smart contracts' code can be read by anyone, every contractor can be sure that they're getting exactly the money they deserve, thus reducing the pain of reconciliation. The actual royalty payment process was also streamlined; each contractor and publisher got their own "address," and smart contracts started automatically moving money between addresses each time a sale was made.[42]

The upshot was that Xbox reduced the royalty settlement time from 45 days to minutes, letting publishers get real-time insights and make adjustments to contracts on the fly. Xbox's finance team also reduced its workload by 70% and reduced the time needed to onboard new publishers from multiple days to 15 minutes.[43] In short, this blockchain solution was a win-win-win for Xbox, publishers, and contracts.

Cloud blockchain and big data

Xbox didn't build the whole blockchain system itself, though. It didn't create its own nodes, install servers to store the blockchain, and write all the necessary code. Instead, it turned to Microsoft's cloud-computing arm, Azure, and used Azure's *blockchain-as-a-service* feature.[44] Xbox got to use Azure's pre-built blockchain code, store blockchains on Azure's supercomputers, and use Azure's security and reliability features. This way, Xbox could avoid the overhead cost and maintenance headache that would come with running a blockchain itself — no need to reinvent the wheel!

What's more, storing all data in a blockchain forces it to be in a single, structured format. Before, when information was scattered across myriad papers and documents, analyzing it was nearly impossible; just finding and cleaning the data would have taken ages. (Anyone who's ever tried to cross-reference data between three different Excel sheets knows how much better it is to have everything in a similar format.) Now that data is in a single format, publishers can easily pull it into data analysis and visualization software to understand, say, how their music payments have grown over time and where they can cut costs.[45] Plus, having large amounts of *structured data* like this makes machine learning much easier, helping unlock more insights.[46]

As you can see, blockchain technology has a remarkable amount of overlap with some of the other hot technology trends: cloud computing, big data, and machine learning. That's no accident; each of these technologies feeds off the others, and they work best when used together.

The masters of private blockchains

If we step back and take a broader look at these private blockchain success stories, one surprising fact jumps out: the groups that have had the most success with private blockchains have not been scrappy startups but rather behemoths like Walmart, IBM, Microsoft, and stock exchanges. Nobody would bat an eye if a small grocer or startup announced it was putting its supply chain on the blockchain, but when Walmart makes the same announcement, people around the world take notice.

This is especially odd when you consider how strongly the crypto space emphasizes startups and the disruption of incumbents. Why have big, slow-moving incumbents gained so much from a "disruptive" technology like private blockchains?

We'd argue it's because implementing a private blockchain isn't really a technical challenge at all; it's a social challenge. The blockchains used by Walmart, the ASX, and Xbox aren't much more complex than Bitcoin's or Ethereum's, and cloud blockchain offerings like Azure's make it easy to set up a blockchain even if you have little prior knowledge. Building the blockchains has been the easy part. In all three cases we explored, the hard part has been the people part: Walmart needed to get all its suppliers to buy into an untested new technology, the ASX had to maintain legal compliance and keep traders calm as they switched to a brand-new system, and Xbox had to teach all its publishers and accountants about the blockchain-based tool.

Big companies, for all their slowness in picking up new technologies, are very good at these people problems. They are much better than startups at getting large groups of people to change their behavior — Walmart can force suppliers to track produce on a blockchain, while a tiny new grocer probably couldn't. They have enough lawyers to make sure they can comply with regulations, as in ASX's case; startups usually can't keep up.[47] And when they do adopt new technologies, they can deploy them at a broad enough scale that they can save enough to offset the up-front cost; Xbox stands to gain a lot more from the efficiency of blockchain-based royalty payments than a startup studio.

Startups may have better blockchain technology, but for most private blockchain projects, it's not the technology that matters — it's getting adoption, getting people comfortable with change, and working out all the legal and financial difficulties that come up. This is a space where established players have an edge, as we've seen throughout this chapter.

Chapter 7.
Cryptocurrency Policy

When Bitcoin currency is converted from currency into cash, that interface has to remain under some regulatory safeguards. I think the fact that within the bitcoin universe an algorithm replaces the function of the government ...[that] is actually pretty cool.
> —Al Gore, former Vice President of the United States[1]

Surprisingly for a technology widely associated with illegality, fraud, and distrust of governments, the path to trusted blockchains runs through governance, regulation, and law.
> —Kevin Werbach, author of *The Blockchain and the New Architecture of Trust*[2]

ONE BIG DRAW of cryptocurrencies early on was the total lack of regulation around them — you could maintain some amount of anonymity, avoid taxes,[3] invest without having to file paperwork,[4] send money anywhere without the red tape,[5] and so on.

But that wasn't because cryptocurrencies exist outside the scope of regulation — in fact, because cryptocurrencies affect the heavily-regulated financial space, they are prime candidates for regulation.[6] It was just that cryptocurrencies operated under the radar for several years, and once they came into the public eye, lawmakers were caught flat-footed. But now that lawmakers have had time to understand the implications of this rapid technological advance, they've begun crafting and enforcing policies around cryptocurrencies.[7]

Crypto bans

By design, cryptocurrencies flout a lot of the careful regulations that governments have put in place around the financial system. Traditional ways of holding and moving money — credit cards, checks, stocks, real estate purchases, you name it — always attach your name to the transaction. But cryptocurrencies don't.

This makes it much easier to launder money: normally you'd need to do complicated things like setting up long links of shell companies[8] or making big real estate purchases,[9] but with cryptocurrencies it's as easy as finding an exchange that doesn't ask for identification. You just buy coins with dirty dollars, move the money between a few different cryptocurrencies, and then cash out for "clean" dollars. You could also send money to a *tumbler*, which combines your cryptocoins with others' and hands you back coins at random from the pool, thus making it difficult to track your money's history.[10]

Since names aren't attached to transactions, cryptocurrencies also make tax evasion easy[11] and make tracing payments far harder — which is why cybercriminals love demanding payment in cryptocurrencies[12] and using them for illegal drug sales.[13]

The simplest solution to these regulatory headaches is to ban cryptocurrencies outright, and that's exactly what many countries have done. Russia,[14] Thailand,[15] Vietnam,[16] Ecuador,[17] Bolivia,[18] Bangladesh,[19] and Kyrgyzstan[20] outright banned all use of cryptocurrencies in the mid-2010s, focusing on Bitcoin's frequent use in money laundering,[21] drug trafficking, and tax evasion.[22] Taiwan forbade Bitcoin after a Hong Kong tycoon was kidnapped and held hostage for millions of dollars in Bitcoin.[23]

These knee-jerk reactions come with downsides, though. Cryptocurrencies have plenty of legitimate uses and can help the economy if harnessed properly. Thus, many larger countries have taken more nuanced approaches; the US's general approach has been to treat cryptocurrencies just like any other store of value (dollars, property, stocks, cars, etc.) and apply the same kind of regulations.[24]

China's Bitcoin drama

China is an interesting case study because of its seeming love-hate relationship with cryptocurrencies. As we've mentioned throughout this book, China is a huge player in the Bitcoin space: 80% of bitcoins are mined there,[25] some of the biggest and most influential mining pools are there,[26] and it produces many of the most popular ASICs.[27]

At the same time, China has placed heavy bans on much of the Bitcoin ecosystem. China banned financial institutions like banks from handling Bitcoin in 2013, but private citizens were apparently still allowed to use bitcoins.[28] The country banned cryptocurrency exchanges in 2017,[29] but citizens just started using *virtual private networks* (*VPNs*) to access Japan- or Hong Kong-based exchanges instead.[30]

China really stepped up its efforts in 2018, when it instructed government task forces to "guide the shutdown" of mining operations, though it didn't give a timetable for the shutdown.[31] That same year, it banned all Chinese citizens from trading cryptocurrencies, including in foreign exchanges.[32]

China's approach to Bitcoin is indeed strange; it benefits greatly from dominating the Bitcoin space, yet it also wants to shut it down.[33] Some people suspect this is because China wants to develop its own cryptocurrency, so it wants to grow the crypto space in general while taking down Bitcoin, which would be the biggest competitor to this hypothetical Chinese cryptocurrency.[34]

The difficulty of regulation

The fact that Bitcoin is still thriving in China despite the (very powerful) government's heavy restrictions shows that cryptocurrency regulations are difficult to enforce.

Because cryptocurrency users are tech-savvy, often more so than regulators, any individual nation's attempts to crack down on currencies don't always work since traders and miners can easily shift operations to more permissive areas. After the US started cracking down on crypto startups in 2018, many such startups considered moving to Switzerland, a place with a much more pro-crypto regulatory environment.[35]

And while China may have soured on miners, places like northern Quebec[36] and Mongolia,[37] which have cheap electricity and need the economic boost from mining, have been somewhat friendlier to miners.

In our opinion, unilateral crypto regulations just shift crypto activity to other countries. Significant change will only happen if countries start teaming up to make multinational accords to crack down on cryptocurrencies.

Venezuela's state-backed cryptocurrency

Venezuela was in the midst of a political and economic crisis in 2018, with inflation topping 60,000% a year[38] — that means that prices more than doubled every month, obliterating savings and businesses. A loaf of bread would cost 6,000 times as much on December 31st as it did on January 1st. At the same time, strongman President Nicolas Maduro's government was getting hammered by international sanctions,[39] making it ever harder to dig out of the hole.

In December 2017, Maduro announced the creation of a cryptocurrency called the Petro, which he said would be backed by Venezuela's oil and mineral reserves.[40] He promised to peg one Petro to the value of a barrel of oil and back it with oil reserves in the rural Venezuelan region of Ayacucho.[41]

Maduro doubled down on the move in August 2018, announcing a new paper currency called the sovereign bolivar that was worth 100,000 old bolivars. The sovereign bolivar would also be linked to the Petro; 3600 new bolivars could be exchanged for one Petro, according to Maduro.[42]

The scam

The problem is that the Petro is a complete scam. For one, the Petro isn't really backed by oil in that you can't exchange a Petro for a barrel of oil — Venezuelans will just be able to pay taxes in Petro at an exchange rate determined by oil prices.[43] (And when you consider that Venezuela considered pre-selling Petro tokens for a 60% discount, you begin to wonder if it could really be tied to the price of oil.[44]) The Ayacucho region, which contains the oil reserves that supposedly back the Petro, has no oil-related activity, and all oil rigs in the area are decrepit and abandoned.[45]

Ayacucho, shown here, is located in the Orinoco oil-producing region of Venezuela. Maduro claims that the oil here will back the Petro, but it's abandoned. Source: The Energy Consulting Group[46] and Scribble Maps[47]

The Petro isn't even a functioning currency. It has never been used, no major cryptocurrency exchange sells it, and no shops accept it.[48] The only scrap of evidence that the Petro even exists is an Ethereum-based token called the Petro that has 100 million active tokens, which is the same number of tokens that Maduro promised. Nobody has ever traded these tokens, though, and it's not clear if these are the same Petros that Maduro was referring to.[49]

The currency was already questionable back in its pre-sale days. The whitepaper behind the currency was light on details and was highly inconsistent, changing its story about which blockchain platform it would use: one day it said it would be built atop Ethereum and use ERC-20 tokens, and another day it said it would use the competing platform NEM.[50] Maduro said he raised several billion dollars from the presale of Petro, but economics professor Steve Hanke says these claims are laughable and have never been audited.[51]

And finally, the Petro is an awful investment. Foreigners can't do anything with it,[52] and the Venezuelan government has a history of devaluing currency and setting arbitrary exchange rates.[53]

Sanction evasion

So why would Maduro launch such an obviously fraudulent cryptocurrency? It was most likely a way to get around US-led sanctions. Venezuela had $140 billion in debt when the Petro was announced,[54] but sanctions prevented foreigners from investing legally in Venezuela.[55] Maduro probably realized that a cryptocurrency, thanks to its untraceability, would let people invest money in Venezuela without the sanctioning countries noticing. The Petro sought to raise $6 billion,[56] which would have made a small but not insignificant dent in the country's debt.

The fundraising attempt was, of course, a failure. As the *Washington Post* put it, "it's just a way for Caracas to try to get around the sanctions against it while raising money from the only people more clueless than itself."[57]

The moral of the story is that governments' relationships with cryptocurrencies cut both ways: cryptocurrencies may break a country's financial laws, but they can also help countries get around international financial laws they don't like. In fact, other countries under sanctions, including Russia, Turkey, and Iran, have looked into raising money through state-issued cryptocurrencies as well.[58]

It's troubling that rogue governments can use cryptocurrencies to circumvent international laws and treaties.[59] Again, this capability is baked into cryptocurrencies: they make it easy for anyone to send money anywhere, and they deliberately make tracing payments difficult. This is very convenient for legitimate money transfers, but it's also helpful for illegal money movements like sanction avoidance. Since anyone can create a new cryptocurrency, there's no single cryptocurrency that international lawmakers can attack. Instead, international governing bodies need to proactively regulate any and all cryptocurrencies if they want to stop illegal actions like these.

ICOs and scams

When a new company wants to raise large amounts of money, it starts selling shares of stock to the public in an *initial public offering,* or *IPO.*[60] Owning shares entitles you to a slice of the company's profits and (sometimes) voting power in corporate decisions. As the company grows, the demand for a slice of profits, and hence the stock price, rises. So when you buy stocks in an IPO, you're betting that the company will grow, that the stock price will rise, and that you'll make a profit.[61]

Getting to an IPO is incredibly difficult, though — it takes years of paperwork, intense scrutiny by regulators and auditors, and countless sales pitches to potential investors.[62] And, these days, tech startups are staying private longer and longer,[63] meaning that only venture capitalists can invest in startups for most of their high-growth early years — everyday investors are locked out until the IPO, at which point much of the company's growth is behind it.[64]

So the crypto world has created a parallel to IPOs, known as *initial coin offerings*, or *ICOs*. ICOs let a blockchain- or cryptocurrency-based startup offer crypto-tokens for sale early in the startup's life, thus letting the startup raise money and letting investors bet on the startup's success.[65] ICOs offer tokens to raise money for a crypto startup; IPOs offer shares of stock to raise money for a traditional startup.

Of securities and utilities

There are two major types of ICOs: those offering *security tokens* and those offering *utility tokens*.[66] Security tokens work pretty much the same as stocks: the startup hands you these tokens (tracked on a blockchain) and you get voting power and sometimes a share of the company's profits. Like stocks, the demand for security tokens, and thus their price, goes up if investors think the company is going to grow.[67]

Utility tokens are unique: you buy the tokens that are used to pay for the startup's services. (If the startup offers its own cryptocurrency, it'll sell those cryptocoins instead of tokens.) For instance, FileCoin (the decentralized file-storage app we talked about earlier) offered FIL coins in its ICO,[68] which you would use to pay other users to store files for you.[69] In its ICO, Ethereum sold ether (or ETH coins), which is the currency you use to pay to run DApps.[70] As the service gets more popular, the demand for the token or coin, and hence their price should rise. So when you buy into a utility token ICO, you're betting that the service will get more popular. Another plus is that you're pre-buying access to the service for a lower price than it would cost later, saving you money if you intend to use the service heavily.[71]

Imagine if a gumball machine only accepted a certain kind of arcade token, and there were only a fixed number of these arcade tokens out there. If the gumballs became popular, the price of tokens would rise as more and more people wanted them. If you bought a bunch of tokens early on for 25¢ and the price eventually rose to $1, you'd be in luck — you could either sell those tokens for 75¢ of profit each, or you could use those tokens to buy gumballs and save yourself 75¢ per gumball.

In this example, you'd buy the gumball tokens early on (the equivalent of the ICO) if you either wanted to use the gumball machine a lot or if you just wanted an investment that you could profit from. This means that a utility token's price is determined by two things: the value of the service itself and also investors' opinions of the company's success.[72] The second determinant is shared with security tokens; remember this, since it'll be important for legal considerations later.

Either type of ICO is viable, though utility tokens are generally more common than security tokens.[73] We imagine this is because they give crypto-startups two ways to grow their tokens' or coins' price: either improving the service or gaining buzz among investors.

Good, bad, and scammy

It's remarkably easy to launch an ICO: all you need is a whitepaper describing your startup idea[74] and some buzz. There's no regulation, and anyone, anywhere can buy tokens and support your idea. Whether ICOs offer security or utility tokens, they offer a cheaper, faster,[75] and red tape-free way to raise money.[76]

ICOs also let everyday investors invest early in startups' lifecycles, making them as open and accessible as Kickstarter projects.[77] Compare that to traditional companies, where everyday investors can only get in late, after the IPO.

But the ease of launching ICOs is also their undoing. Without the extensive oversight of an IPO, there's little to stop scammers from running amok. A full 80% of ICOs are estimated to be scams,[78] and from 2016 to 2018 ICO scams stole almost $100 million from everyday investors.[79]

When you invest in an ICO, usually you have little to go off besides the whitepaper. You trust that the company will deliver on the promises it made in the whitepaper; only then will the tokens you bought gain value. But companies often fail to live up to their promises, and worse, there's nothing stopping a fraudulent company from taking the ICO funds and running without even building the product. This scam is known as an *exit scam*:[80] it's when a company raises money based on a whitepaper but disappears before building anything.

Hundreds of ICOs have turned out to be exit scams.[81] One notorious one was called LoopX, a cryptocurrency investment startup that offered a vague "investment platform" that would deliver "guaranteed profits every week" to investors. (Yeah, right.) LoopX raised $4.5 million from its ICO but the company vanished in February 2018. Its website and social media all disappeared from the internet.[82] This $4.5 million heist was the *fifth* major ICO fraud of 2018, and it only happened in February![83]

Even established crypto startups can take users' money and run, and there's little anyone can do about it. The most famous crypto-startup to run a scam like this was called BitConnect. BitConnect was an investment platform that promised a 1% return every day and guaranteed investors a 40% total return every month. That means that $1,000 invested today would become $50 million in 3 years.[84]

This business model was quickly flagged as suspicious,[85] but that didn't stop BitConnect from hitting a $2.6 billion market cap after its 2016 ICO. Throughout 2017, the company ran an aggressive marketing campaign, bragging about the "profits" it had earned investors, but BitConnect hadn't really invested anything — the "returns" investors got was just money that newer investors had put in! (This is the textbook definition of a pyramid scheme.)[86]

In January 2018, the company suddenly shut down without a trace. The value of the BitConnect cryptocurrency, which BitConnect was built on, plunged 96%. Many investors had put their life savings in BitConnect — and they were ruined.[87] Meanwhile, the BitConnect owners sold all their coins for hefty sums of money right before the company shut down; they vanished right after.[88]

Had BitConnect been a traditional company, it probably never would have made it past IPO, since regulators and auditors would have quickly realized the company had all the markings of a scam. But without any gatekeepers, BitConnect could flourish.

The lack of regulation around ICOs also lets more conventional criminals raise money without law enforcement noticing. In 2018, the infamous Macau gangster named Wan Kuok-Koi launched an ICO for the "HB" coin, which he said he would award as prizes in poker tournaments. Wan, who served 14 years in prison for illegal gambling and loansharking,[89] raised over $750 million in the first 5 minutes of this sale.[90] (This is somewhat like the Petro case: a man whom no legitimate institution would ever lend to managed to raise funds anyway using a shady new cryptocurrency.)

The notorious Macau gangster Wan Kuok-Koi, who raised $750 million in 5 minutes after launching a shady cryptocurrency. Source: South China Morning Post[91]

In short, ICOs suffer from the classic cryptocurrency problem: removing all gatekeepers makes innovation faster and easier, but it also enables scammers and criminals. It's an interesting new way to raise capital, but you can't help but think that the scammers have the upper hand.

ICO regulation

The reason ICOs were able to avoid scrutiny for so long was that cryptocurrencies and tokens weren't treated as *securities*. The US Securities and Exchange Commission (the SEC) heavily regulates the sale of securities. Stocks are classified as securities, which is why IPOs face so much regulation from the SEC.[92]

The disturbing number of scams and criminal activity associated with ICOs makes them a ripe target for regulation. But is there a legal reason to regulate them?

Securities

When it comes to ICO regulation, the big question is: are tokens and cryptocoins securities? If they are, then ICOs can and should be regulated just like IPOs.[93]

The SEC has a longstanding test, known as the *Howey test*, to check if an asset is a security. The test says that an investment is a security if "a person invests his money in a common enterprise and is led to expect profits solely from the efforts of the promoter or a third party."[94]

Basically, if you invest in a company hoping that the company's work will bring you profits, you've just bought a security.[95] This is the definition of a stock, so stocks are clearly securities.

How about ICOs? Remember that ICOs sell one of two types of tokens: security tokens and utility tokens. Security tokens are definitely securities — it's in their name. They work just like stocks — you buy coins or tokens that grow in value when the company grows — so they clearly can be regulated like stocks.

Utility tokens are a more complex case. Recall that there are two reasons why you might buy a utility token: to pay upfront to use a service before it gets expensive, or because you want to sell the tokens for more money as the service gets more popular. In the first case, the utility token isn't a security, since you aren't expecting a profit; you just want to save money. In the second case, the utility token behaves a lot like security tokens or stocks: you're investing in the company and hoping it grows so you can profit. So the utility token *is* a security in this case.

So, legally, where does that leave utility tokens? Blockchain lawyer Marco Santori said that pre-sale utility tokens are securities because they are primarily used for investments (just as stocks you buy in an IPO are investments). But he argues that, after launch, a utility token is not a security, since you'd primarily buy it to use the service, not as an investment.[96] We would argue that people still use utility tokens as investments post-launch, though: ether is a utility token since you use it to run Ethereum DApps, and though ether has been available for years, people still use it for investment and speculation.[97]

So our take is that both types of ICO tokens are securities since people will always use them for investments. Thus, they should be regulated like stocks.

The SEC's crackdown

The SEC came to a similar conclusion and announced in 2017 that ICO tokens were securities and would start being regulated as such.[98] ICOs would be banned in the United States; crypto-startups hoping to get American investors would have to make a *Security Token Offering*, or *STO*, which is similar to an ICO but gets regulated similarly to an IPO.[99] More generally, cryptocurrencies would be regulated similarly to stocks.[100]

This was bad news for startups that liked using ICOs as unregulated ways to raise funds.[101] They had two choices: either keep their ICOs and just ban Americans from participating, or go through the legal and regulatory work of getting an STO. Many startups chose the first option since it's less hassle.[102]

There are several ways for a crypto-startup to get approval for an STO:[103]

- Formally register the offering with the SEC. This requires most of the same scrutiny as an IPO, so it's very hard and expensive. Crypto-startups at the time of their ICO are usually far smaller than regular startups at the time of their IPO, so this option is prohibitive for most crypto-startups. Most crypto-startups seeking to do an STO look for an exemption, which would let them legally launch an STO without having to register with the SEC.[104]

- Use an exemption called Regulation D 506(c), or Reg D. Reg D says that you don't have to file with the SEC if you only sell to *accredited investors*.[105] This term refers to investors or companies with enough wealth and knowledge that the SEC thinks they're capable of handling risky crypto investments. Investors can become accredited by having an income over $200,000, having a net worth over $1 million, being a registered broker or investment advisor, or having other professional or educational experience that proves they know what they're doing.[106] Reg D is quite easy to use: companies seeking to do an ICO can just say "accredited investors only in the US," and they can instantly get a Reg D-compliant STO. Thus, it's probably the most popular exemption.[107]

- Use an exemption called Regulation Crowdfunding, or Reg CF.[108] This lets any investor (accredited or unaccredited) participate, but the startup can only raise about $1 million a year with this method.[109] The fundraising cap is so low that this regulation is not terribly useful.

- Use Regulation A+, which lets anyone participate, like Reg CF, but has a fundraising cap of $50 million. However, the offering must be approved by the SEC, which is quite rigorous and difficult.[110] Reg A+ is generally considered better but harder to obtain than Reg D, so it's reserved for larger crypto-startups.[111]

When creating an STO, a crypto-startup will usually choose one of the exemptions (usually Reg D) to sell to US-based investors and use a separate exemption called Regulation S to sell to investors abroad. Reg S says, in essence, that a company can raise unlimited amounts of money from any investor abroad as long as it uses certain approved practices.[112] This is why you may hear about Reg D/S or Reg A+/S STOs.

	Need SEC approval?	Investor restrictions	Fundraising cap
Register with SEC	Yes, with add'l scrutiny	None	None
Reg CF	No	None	$1 million
Reg D	No	Accredited investors only	None
Reg A+	Yes	None	$50 million

The main methods of creating an STO in the US. Each has its drawbacks.

Exchanges need to do extra work for STOs as well. Exchanges offering STO tokens or cryptocoins for sale have to do *know your customer* (*KYC*) and *anti-money laundering* (*AML*) checks on buyers — basically checking to be sure that real humans are buying the tokens, not robots, and that these humans aren't criminals.[113] This is very time-intensive and expensive for exchanges,[114] but the big-name exchanges have implemented them.[115] (Incidentally, KYC and AML checks are why you now have to upload pictures of your passport or driver's license when you sign up for an account on Coinbase or other exchanges.[116])

A review of STOs

STOs give crypto-startups a choice: either register your offering with the SEC like a traditional IPO, or don't register but only sell to people who know what they're doing (accredited investors). This means that unaccredited American investors can't invest in non-vetted STOs — which protects less-wealthy and less-informed investors from participating in what is basically high-stakes crypto-gambling. (This is a real problem: many new investors take advances on their credit cards just to buy cryptocurrencies — meaning they're gambling with money they don't even have. This SEC regulation, for better or for worse, aims to protect these people.[117]) In general, the STO seems like a fair middle ground between allowing free-for-all ICOs and totally shutting down crypto-fundraising.

On the flipside, STOs make early-stage investing in crypto impossible for everyday investors; ICOs were supposed to solve this problem, but STOs are no better than IPOs in this regard.[118] Another critique is that the legal burden could become crushing if every country adopted its own STO rules — abiding by the US's restrictions is hard enough, but having to comply with dozens would be too hard for fledgling crypto-startups.[119]

As time goes on, we expect crypto-fundraising to look more and more similar to traditional IPO fundraising. That means that all the benefits and drawbacks of the old approach — some of which we've touched on here — will continue showing up in the crypto space.

Chapter 8.

What's Next

Bitcoin is just one example of something that uses a blockchain. Cryptocurrencies are just one example of decentralized technologies… I think decentralized networks will be the next huge wave in technology. The blockchain allows our smart devices to speak to each other better and faster.

—Melanie Swan, author of *Blockchain: Blueprint for a New Economy*[1]

I really like Bitcoin… It's a store of value, a distributed ledger. It's also a good investment vehicle if you have an appetite for risk. But it won't be a currency until volatility slows down.

—David Marcus, former CEO of PayPal[2]

THESE DAYS, the crypto space is dominated by startup currencies and corporate back-office tools. But it won't always be like that. The role and scope of crypto seems set to expand substantially, and interestingly, it may not even use blockchains anymore.

Facebook's Diem

In June 2019, former PayPal head David Marcus, then the head of Facebook's cryptocurrency division, unveiled Facebook Libra (later renamed Diem[3]), a new stablecoin that it would run with 27 partners, including Visa, eBay, Uber, and, yes, PayPal.[4]

This was a bold move for the social networking company, but hardly a surprise, since it had been rumored for years that Facebook would be adding a stablecoin to WhatsApp[5] and Messenger.[6]

The app for everything

Diem was designed for use on Facebook's messaging apps (though it was technically independent from Facebook), merchants could accept it as payment, and users could convert it to and from fiat currencies through an exchange. But why would a social networking company get into crypto?

The most obvious reason was that it would help Facebook track exactly what people were spending money on, which would be extremely valuable data for advertisers — thus helping Facebook target ads better and charge a higher price for ads.[7]

But, second, Facebook had long shown interest in evolving from a social network to *the* app for all economic activity.[8] The role model here was the Chinese app WeChat: originally a texting app, it started letting people pay their friends in 2014. It hooked people on the feature by letting people send digital money packets for Lunar New Year, digitizing a popular Chinese tradition.[9] Once it had hundreds of millions of people's payment information, it started letting people do everything from hailing taxis to paying bills to buying movie tickets[10] to paying rent.[11] (You're much more likely to buy a movie ticket on an app if you already entered your credit card information in the app!)

WeChat is China's app for everything,[12] and Facebook made no secret that it wanted to become the *world's* app for everything.[13][14] Step one of this plan would be to get everyone using Facebook to send money.

International payments

Facebook's first goal with Diem was to serve the market for *remittances*, or money that people send home to developing countries.[15]

This makes sense on the surface. WhatsApp is phenomenally popular in the developing markets that use remittances the most: India, WhatsApp's biggest market,[16] receives over $70 billion in remittances every year.[17]

But why crypto? You've long been able to pay friends on Messenger,[18] and in 2019, Facebook announced Facebook Pay, yet another payment system for Facebook, WhatsApp, and Instagram.[19] What does crypto bring to the table?

It hinges on the difference between domestic and international payments. Sending money inside a country, especially in the US, is pretty streamlined with the conventional financial system. Venmo is free, sending money between American banks is a few dollars at most,[20] using checks costs just a few cents each,[21] and credit cards charge less than 3 percent.[22] And all of these methods take, at worst, two or three business days.

But cross-border payments are a nightmare. Sending money to a bank abroad takes weeks, and it's not uncommon for payments to get lost in transit, money to get held up in security and regulatory checks, poor exchange rates to eat up your payment, and fees over $50 to get slapped on. If you need to send money from, say, the UK to Africa, it's often faster, cheaper, and easier to fly over with a suitcase full of cash.[23]

Blockchain expert Chris Ferris gave a similar example at a talk at South by Southwest: if you wanted to send $10,000 from the US to Indonesia, your bank wouldn't be able to give you an estimated price or arrival date; you may not even know if the money even arrived. Your best bet would be to mail a wad of cash there with UPS — then you'd get insurance and tracking, and you'd know exactly how much you'd pay and when it'd arrive. In short, international payments are awful.

Remittances are especially bad. Sending $200 (a benchmark commonly used for measuring remittance fees) internationally costs $14 on average, while sending $500 costs about $25 — a fee ranging from 5-7%. These fees rack up quickly: Americans spend over $30 billion a year on remittance fees. The problem is so bad that the UN has named reducing remittance fees to below 5% as one of its biggest international development goals.[24]

So, with the traditional financial system, domestic payments are quick and cheap, while international payments are hopelessly broken. The reason crypto is important is that it works the same no matter how much money you're sending or where you're sending it. Whether you're buying a $5 coffee in your local cafe or sending $1,000,000 to Papua New Guinea, paying with Bitcoin takes exactly the same amount of time (about an hour[25]) and costs the exact same amount (about a dollar[26]).

Amount sent within US	Credit card	Bank transfer	Bitcoin
$10	$0.30	Free	$1
$10,000	$300	Free	$1
$10 mil.	Impossible	Free	$1

The approximate costs of sending money through various means within the US.

Amount sent to Indonesia	Mail cash via UPS	Bank transfer	Bitcoin
$10	$30	Impossible	$1
$10,000	$150	$400	$1
$10 mil.	Impossible	$400,000	$1

The approximate costs of sending money through various means from the US to Indonesia.

This means that, compared to the status quo, paying with cryptocurrencies is underwhelming for small domestic payments but game-changing for large or international payments. Cryptocurrencies are far, far better than the status quo for sending money internationally, which is exactly why Facebook, which is seeing most of its growth coming from the developing world,[27] is so keen on using Diem for payments.

Struggles

The business case for Diem makes sense, and its design managed to avoid a lot of the pitfalls that usually trip up cryptocurrencies. Diem is pegged to a basket of fiat currencies,[28] thus reducing its volatility and making it a suitable candidate for payments. Facebook and its partners hold almost total control over Diem's future, thus reducing the risk of rebellions or hard forks splintering the currency.[29]

However, Facebook quickly ran into problems. US Senators grilled Marcus about Diem, saying it was "delusional" to trust Facebook with people's money.[30] The media and the public were skeptical of Diem given their widespread distrust of Facebook's privacy practices.[31] And, worst of all, the major payment processors that partnered with Facebook to launch the coin, including Visa, Mastercard, Stripe, eBay, and PayPal, all quit within just a few months of the currency's announcement.[32]

But why? It might be that Diem was trying to have it all. Crypto enthusiasts were turned off by Diem's centralization of power in the hands of major tech and finance companies — the exact opposite of cryptocurrencies' usual ethos of democratization, decentralization, and cutting out financial middlemen.[33]

Meanwhile, payment processors were afraid of running afoul of strict fraud and money-laundering laws, which Diem seemed to want to avoid whenever possible.[34] They were, no doubt, spooked by a letter that two US Senators sent to them:

> *Facebook appears to want the benefits of engaging in financial activities without the responsibility of being regulated as a financial services company... If you take this on, you can expect a high level of scrutiny from regulators not only on Libra-related activities, but on all payment activities.*[35]

The verdict

Diem is an ambitious project — perhaps too ambitious for the time when it launched. The regulation wasn't yet in place, nobody knew the right model for how private companies could and should use cryptocurrencies, and most of Facebook's finance-industry partners weren't ready to take the plunge. Libra's future remains to be seen, but it's clear that it won't be easy.

Looking at the bigger picture, Diem is the prime example of how cryptocurrencies are being used in ways antithetical to their founding spirit. Bitcoin was invented to cut out middlemen, work around banks, make transactions transparent, and give average users a way to earn money and be part of the currency's future (as via mining). Diem is the exact opposite: it's run by gargantuan tech and finance companies, all payments and data will flow through Facebook,[36] the blockchain may not be publicly viewable,[37] and ordinary users get no say in its future. [38]

Is this a betrayal of crypto's values? Or just the cost of trying to go mainstream? That's a judgment call, but it at least shows that cryptocurrencies aren't all the same.

Tokenization

Many people view the future of currency as a battle between cryptocurrencies and fiat currencies, but that's not an accurate division. It's actually possible for fiat currencies to adopt some elements of cryptocurrencies through a process called *tokenization*, or when a country starts representing its currency as cryptocoins.[39]

A thought experiment should make it clearer. Suppose the Fed announced a new AmeriCoin (with a short name of AMC), a cryptocoin that you could buy from the Fed for $1 each or sell to the Fed for $1 each. Currently, banks, credit card companies, investment accounts, and other financial institutions represent account balances as just numbers in a database. But in this world, these institutions would actually hold AMC. When your employer paid you, it would send AMC to your bank account, which would hold your AMC in a wallet. When you went to pay your credit card payment, you'd have your bank send AMC to the credit card company. If you wanted, say, a car loan, the lender would send AMC to your bank's wallet and perhaps set up a smart contract that would automatically deduct AMC from your bank's wallet every month as interest payments.

At a more macro scale, when the Fed wants to increase or decrease the amount of money in circulation, it buys or sells bonds to/from banks.[a] Currently, the Fed keeps an internal ledger of how much money each participating bank has, and when it buys or sells bonds, it just updates the banks' credit totals — no cash actually exchanges hands.[40] In this new world, the Fed might actually send AMC to or from banks in exchange for bonds (which might also be represented as crypto-tokens).

If the government really wanted to push adoption of AMC, it could even allow (or require) Americans to pay taxes by sending AMC to the IRS. (It's said that governments can make their money have value by forcing people to pay taxes with it;[41] in this case, it could encourage or force people to use AMC.)

The limited effects of tokenization

This new world of tokenized US dollars might behave very differently under the surface — with transactions using cryptocoins under the hood — but it wouldn't change all that much at the surface. For average residents, there might be a small

---

[a] See Appendix B to learn more about monetary policy and other macroeconomic concepts.

gain in efficiency since all financial institutions would be automatically compatible — no more hassle moving money between accounts, investments, and loans.

The government might gain a few benefits.[42] (Few people have thought hard about how currency tokenization would actually work,[43] so this is mostly speculation.) Depending on the setup of the AmeriCoin, the government may be able to track more transactions to crack down on tax evasion and get a better sense for the state of the economy. It would also force a much-needed modernization of government and industry banking systems, which are still built with an ancient programming language known as COBOL — a language that was a hot new thing back in 1960.[44] Getting everyone to use a blockchain would probably improve security and prevent crippling failures as COBOL continues to age.

While tokenization might lead to some efficiency and security improvements, it probably wouldn't change the structure of the economy. As an analogy, consider when the US switched from the gold standard — when all dollars could be converted to and from gold — to fiat money between 1933 and 1971.[45] The move off the gold standard made the economy more stable because the government could freely create or destroy money when the economy was too weak or too strong, respectively — it's much easier to create bonds out of thin air and sell them than to create gold out of thin air! But, regardless, most economic structures stayed the same: there were still banks, paper money, the Fed, loans, credit cards, and so on.[46]

Similarly, even if everyone pays for things with AMC instead of paper money or bank transfers, all those financial institutions will need to stick around. People will still need to be able to take out loans. People will still want the fraud protection and ability to dispute payments of credit cards.[47] The Fed will still need to change the amount of money in the economy (*monetary policy*) to keep the economy humming. And people will still want to save and invest money using banks, stocks, and so on. The form that these institutions take may change, but the institutions will remain.

The $100,000 bill

We think it's quite likely that countries will tokenize their currencies in the coming decades — tokenization would probably take a lot of work, but it can improve efficiency and security, and there's not much downside to tokenizing. But it won't be as momentous as you might think — the structure of the financial system will stay pretty similar.

While our thought experiment mentioned that consumers might deal with the hypothetical AmeriCoin, we don't think that's feasible in practice. The average person won't want to deal with the hassle of wallets, long private keys, irreversible transactions, and such.[48] The current financial system is confusing enough as is. Instead, we think cryptocurrencies will primarily be used behind the scenes, such as for transactions between banks or for large payments between companies.

This draws a strong parallel to the $100,000 bills used in the US in the 1900s. These were never for consumer use — nobody would have a good reason to have a $100,000 bill, and keeping that much money in cash would be an accident (or robbery) waiting to happen. Instead, they were only used for large transactions between banks, such as if the Fed needed to send large amounts of money to a participating bank after buying bonds.[49]

A $100,000 bill from the 1900s. It was only used for bank-to-bank transfers. Source: BradC via Reddit[50]

In other words, cryptocurrencies' role in currency will be similar to that of the $100,000 bill of the 1900s: boosting efficiency behind the scenes, but far out of the reach of everyday consumers.

China's yuan tokenization

When we spoke with Wharton professor and blockchain scholar Kevin Werbach, he quickly named one country that would be especially interested in tokenizing its currency: China.

We agree with his intuition. China has made no secret that it's trying to make its yuan the world's primary reserve currency.[51] Reserve currencies are the lingua franca of currencies: countries around the world use reserve currencies to pay off international debts, buy commodities like gold and oil, and trade with other countries.[52] The International Monetary Fund (IMF) has an elite list of the world's top reserve currencies: the US dollar, the euro, the British pound, the Japanese yen, and — as of 2016 — the Chinese yuan.[53]

China's addition to that club was great news for the country, because it was a stamp of approval from the International Monetary Fund (which decides the list of reserve currencies), it helped China integrate deeper into the global financial market,[54] and it made it easier for China to do business with other countries (since it can now trade with anyone in yuan, instead of having to convert its money).[55] But the US dollar is still the top dog,[56] and China wants to dethrone it as the most popular reserve currency.

Standing out

It's hard for a normal currency to get out of the dollar's shadow, but if China tokenized its currency before anyone else, it could make a compelling case that it was different from the rest and thus merited special attention.

China has also gotten a bad reputation for *devaluing* its currency in recent years.[57] The yuan is pegged to a basket of currencies, and the exchange rate is set by the Chinese government — and Beijing can choose to arbitrarily cut the exchange rate, making each yuan worth less in terms of other currencies.[58] This move increases exports since the same number of dollars can buy more yuan and thus more goods;[59] this helps China's export-oriented economy. This is widely considered unfair, since it gives China an artificial edge and hurts other countries that don't make this unfair move.[60]

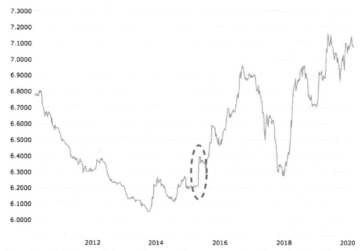

The US Dollar – Chinese Yuan exchange rate over time. China abruptly devalued its currency in August 2015, marked with an oval. It was a small change, but the fact that it was unilateral angered many in the international community. Source: MacroTrends[61]

China's habit of devaluing its currency has made many investors and countries hesitant to embrace it.[62] As long as China can unilaterally decide to devalue its currency, this problem will remain. If China were to create a tokenized yuan that the government physically could *not* devalue (i.e. there was no mechanism for devaluation in the cryptocurrency's source code), that could help the currency gain trust. There's no sign that China is planning to do something this drastic, but it's plausible.

Preparation

There are already some clear signs that China is preparing for a major tokenization effort.

As we've mentioned earlier in the book, the Chinese government used to be lax enough with cryptocurrency to let the crypto space in China blossom; as you'll recall, China thoroughly dominates the Bitcoin economy. But since the mid-2010s, China has been cracking down on cryptocurrencies, making aggressive moves against Bitcoin, banning ICOs,[63] and pushing crypto conferences out of the country.[64]

Where will all the Chinese crypto enthusiasts and companies go if most mainstream cryptocurrencies are banned in China? If China creates its own government-backed cryptocurrency, those crypto enthusiasts will flock right to the government's open arms.

China has also been investing in the technology needed to make this happen. Since 2016, the Chinese national bank has registered at least 78 patents for digital currency, at least 44 of which are related to blockchain. The bank has also been aggressively hiring economists and developers for its new Digital Currency Institute, whose mission is to "issue and distribute a blockchain-based currency."[65] It's hard to think of a more obvious sign that China is taking this seriously.

The only clearer sign is that China has already begun work on prototype cryptocurrencies: in 2017, the country started running cryptocurrency simulations and began testing mock transactions with major Chinese banks.[66]

Our hunch is that China will eventually ban all non-government-controlled cryptocurrencies because it's uneasy about technologies it can't control; most cryptocurrencies are largely out of China's control, and even though the Chinese government and Chinese companies have a large sway over Bitcoin, they can't stop forks or altcoins.

Then we think China will build a prototype tokenized yuan and test it in Africa. China is Africa's largest economic partner and has been investing heavily in infrastructure throughout the continent.[67] Given how volatile African currencies are,[68] large swaths of the continent may welcome the relative transparency and stability of a tokenized yuan. Perhaps China will create a yuan-backed "Afro" currency that is adopted throughout Africa, similar to the euro in Europe.

Once the kinks are worked out in Africa, China could then launch its tokenized yuan in China and then take it around the world. This would set the stage for China's cryptocurrency to become the dominant currency for digital payments and thus, eventually, the world's leading reserve currency. This is all highly speculative, but when you connect all the dots, it's quite possible that this is indeed what China is plotting.

The Internet of Things and going beyond the blockchain

So Facebook and China are rethinking cryptocurrencies as we know them. The *Internet of Things (IoT)*, a term for all the smart devices we use in homes and factories, is forcing us to rethink blockchains as we know them.

IoT's promise and weaknesses

There are all kinds of devices that connect to the internet these days, from Philips Hue smart light bulbs to internet-connected heart monitors to smart toothbrushes.[69] And it's not just consumer products; IoT devices come with smart sensors, which let the devices adapt to their environment and generate massive amounts of data, both of which are very useful for industrial applications. IoT thus has tremendous potential for manufacturing, transportation, cars, healthcare, and more.[70]

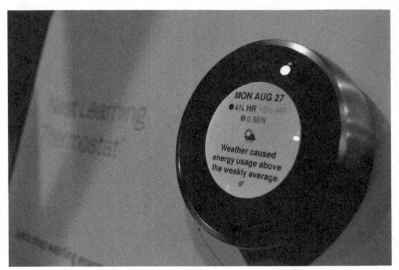

A Nest smart thermostat, one of the most famous IoT devices. Source: Wikimedia[71]

IoT devices' greatest flaw is their lack of security.[72] They've proven surprisingly easy to hack into remotely, and because these devices directly affect the real world, their potential danger is multiplied. There have been some terrifying stories about hackers spying on internet-connected baby cameras,[73] hacked printers reading the contents of confidential documents being printed,[74] and even *Wired* researchers remotely disabling the brakes of a Jeep barreling down a highway.[75] Plus, if someone, say, hacks into a pacemaker and changes the pacemaker's data or source code, the person with that pacemaker could be seriously injured or even killed.[76]

The other big problem is that IoT device networks have traditionally been centralized; most IoT devices can't make many decisions themselves and instead send data to a central server, which makes decisions and tells the devices what to do. This adds all the familiar problems with middlemen: there's a lot of expensive overhead, communications are slow, and the whole system can collapse if the central server goes down or if the connection to the server fails.[77] If you're using thousands of IoT devices that work together to build a car,[78] you definitely do not want to bet everything on the security and reliability of a single server.

In other words, for IoT to succeed, IoT devices need a secure, tamper-proof, and decentralized way to store, access, and share data.

IoT and blockchain

This is where the blockchain comes in. If you have a bunch of IoT devices that are on a car factory floor, they can all store every bit of data they gather — the current number of parts available, the room temperature, the location of any defects — on a blockchain. Since each IoT device would store its own copy of the blockchain, it would always have the latest information and would be fine if the internet connection briefly failed (while it would be in trouble if it relied entirely on a central server). The machine putting wheels on the chassis would always know exactly what to do.

What's more, because the blockchain is virtually tamper-proof, it's much harder for an attacker to compromise the data on the blockchain. And if the IoT devices are only allowed to run smart contracts — which behave predictably — it's much harder for an attacker to make the IoT devices go rogue. If nobody can tamper with the device's data or behavior, it's pretty safe.

Blockchain's flaws

The blockchain isn't perfect for IoT, though. Imagine if you manufactured pills that could never be stored above 90° F for safety reasons. To monitor it, you'd stick a tiny, internet-connected temperature sensor to the bottle cap. The sensor would constantly monitor the temperature, and, if it ever read a temperature above 90 degrees, it would run a smart contract to add an entry to the blockchain saying that the pills had been improperly stored. This way, everyone involved — from the manufacturer to the doctor to the store to the patient — would know when and where the process failed.[79]

This solution would generate a ton of transactions, though. Each pill bottle sensor would probably measure the temperature once every few minutes and write it to the blockchain. If this solution grew to millions of pill bottles, you'd be adding millions of entries to the blockchain every hour.

But, as we've mentioned before, blockchains just aren't built to handle that kind of scale. Bitcoin can only process about 3 transactions per second;[80] Ethereum can do about 15.[81] Each transaction costs money — at most a dollar or two per transaction,[82] but that gets incredibly expensive if you start making millions of transactions an hour. If you use a private blockchain, you can get around the mining costs, but the limited transaction volume would remain a bottleneck.

The reason blockchains have such limited transaction volume is that only one block can be mined at a time. Since blocks can only fit so many transactions and since the block time is pretty much constant, the maximum number of transactions per second is pretty much set in stone. So you have thousands of people wanting to mine blocks but only one lucky person at a time actually getting to do so. If multiple people mine a block at once, the blockchain forks, which defeats the purpose of having a linear chain of history.

So, for blockchains to really work for IoT, you have to get rid of the linear chain — you have to let multiple people add transactions at the same time. Only then can you process thousands or millions of transactions per second. In other words, to make a blockchain work for IoT, you have to get rid of the blockchain.

The tangle

The started IOTA took on this challenge and created an alternative to the blockchain that was optimized for IoT. This alternative, known as the *tangle*, lets many people add transactions at once. Instead of a single linear chain made of blocks, the tangle connects a bunch of transactions in a spaghetti-like[83] structure:[84]

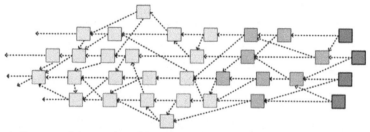

A diagram of the tangle, with newer transactions on the right. Each new transaction verifies two randomly-chosen transactions before it. If a transaction was verified by many later transactions, you can be more certain it was legitimate. In this diagram, brand-new (unverified) transactions are on the right, newly-verified ones are in the middle, and heavily-verified ones are on the left. Source: Wikimedia[85]

The tangle gets rid of mining entirely. To add a transaction to the tangle, you don't have to pay someone who verifies your transaction. Instead, you have to verify two randomly-chosen transactions that came before you. Anyone who makes a transaction effectively serves as a miner for people who made previous transactions. This means that nobody using the tangle has to pay for transactions at all![86]

Since there's no linear list of blocks, an unlimited number of people can add to the tangle at once. You don't even have to know what other people are doing — you just pick two random transactions to verify, regardless of what others are doing. (Compare this to the blockchain, where you always have to be checking what transactions are in the mempool and can be mined.) This is why transactions can be added in parallel.

Since devices don't need to be constantly checking what everyone else is doing, they can still add to the tangle even if they're offline, as long as they can sync up with the tangle later. This is great for IoT devices, which (despite the name) aren't always online.[87]

The tangle manages to offer these benefits while maintaining similar security to the blockchain. Over time, a transaction gets verified by more and more transactions, and the transactions that verify it are themselves verified, and so on. Eventually, a transaction will have a multi-layered "cake" of verified transactions on top of it. The odds of *all* those transactions being wrong or fraudulent becomes quite slim, so you can be pretty confident that the transaction is legitimate.

In short, the tangle has no mining, no fees, infinite scalability, strong security, and less reliance on a perfect internet connection. This makes it ideal for the massive amounts of simultaneous communication that IoT devices need.[88]

Decentralized ledger technology

The tangle example shows that there's more to crypto than just blockchains — there can be all kinds of technologies built on the concept of decentralized ledgers. Other forms of *decentralized ledger technology (DLT)* besides the blockchain and tangle are still emerging, but plenty are possible.

You can even drop the notion of decentralization, as Amazon Web Services' Quantum Ledger Database (QLDB) does. The

QLDB has a central source of truth, thus sacrificing the blockchain's decentralization, but it keeps the blockchain's transparency, immutability, and verification.[89] (QLDB is designed for companies' internal tools; companies are already centralized and thus don't need the decentralization.[90])

At its core, all this technology is really about keeping a detailed, tamper-proof record of history. Using blocks, chains, or even decentralization is ultimately optional.

Chapter 9.

Bubble or Revolution?

Bitcoin is a fraud worse than tulip bulbs... it will eventually blow up.

—Jamie Dimon, CEO of JPMorgan[1]

Still thinking about #Bitcoin. No conclusion - not endorsing/rejecting. Know that folks also were skeptical when paper money displaced gold.

—Lloyd Blankfein, former CEO of Goldman Sachs[2]

IN THIS final chapter, it's time to come full-circle: are blockchains, cryptocurrencies, and related technologies just a bubble, or a bona fide revolution?

The future of money

Bitcoin entrepreneur and Zuckerberg rival Cameron Winklevoss, like many famous crypto backers, argues that cryptocurrencies are "the future of money."[3] In our opinion, it's more complicated than that.

We've already explored tokenization; it may not be that earth-shattering, but it's not a bad idea. So it's quite likely that, over time, countries will start tokenizing parts of their economy. There's ample evidence that China is doing so, and Brazil[4] and Singapore[5] have begun exploring tokenization as well. But a tokenized fiat currency is still, economically speaking, a fiat currency: the government ultimately controls the money, and the money's value is based only on faith in the country's government.

In other words, any government-controlled cryptocurrency is likely to behave similarly to today's fiat currencies. The more interesting question is: will privately-owned cryptocurrencies (Bitcoin, Ethereum, Monero, etc.) replace government-owned currencies? This would be like a return to the gold standard[6] in that the government wouldn't have much control over the economy and that the value of money would be determined by forces outside the government's control.[7]

Citizens' desires

To answer the question, it's helpful to first think of it from a citizen's point of view. Would people want to use, say, Bitcoin for all their financial activities?

There are a couple big red flags with using cryptocurrencies for all financial activity:

○ Cryptocurrencies are worse than current payment methods for small purchases. Since most purchases you make are pretty small, this pain point would be hard to ignore.

○ Payments are irreversible, which makes hacking harder but is also dangerous for consumers. There have already been horror stories of people losing $100,000 when someone hacked into their Coinbase account — and, unlike the conventional financial system, there's absolutely no way to get stolen money back.[8] Many people would not be willing to assume so much risk.

○ Volatility is still a huge problem. So far, all stablecoins have been pegged to fiat currencies.[9] If there are no more fiat currencies, it's hard to see a new way of making stablecoins. Maybe mainstream cryptocurrencies will see a huge decrease in volatility going forward, but that's hard to predict.

○ As Wharton professor Kevin Werbach told us, cryptocurrencies are still too clunky and difficult for the average person to use. Managing private keys and multiple currencies is a hassle. And since one wrong move (like sending bitcoins to a mistyped address) can make your money disappear forever, people can really get in trouble if they misunderstand a single thing about crypto. Indeed, financial illiteracy is already shockingly high in the US: two-thirds of Americans can't calculate interest payments correctly, for instance.[10] Having to use cryptocurrencies would make things even harder for people; currencies should not be so difficult that you have to read a whole book (like this one!) to properly understand them.

In short, most people want a monetary system that just works: it should be stable, forgiving, and easy to use. On all these fronts, crypto loses to our current system. The average person doesn't care much about decentralization. So we wouldn't expect to see entire populations clamoring for cryptocurrencies to replace their government-run currencies.

Countries' desires

So if the case for bottom-up adoption of crypto is weak, how about the case for top-down adoption? Would countries give up control of their currency and make, say, Bitcoin legal tender?

That question answers itself: given a choice, countries wouldn't want to voluntarily give up control over their money. As former Nasdaq EVP John Jacobs explains, if a country made Bitcoin its primary currency, it would become far harder for the central bank to regulate the economy. To avoid sudden price swings, the central bank needs to constantly adjust the total amount of money in circulation, or the *money supply*.[11] The money supply must match the total amount of money residents want to use, or the *money demand*. Money demand goes up during the holiday season as people shop more, and it goes down during recessions.[12]

With a fiat system, central banks like the Fed can easily create or destroy money at will by buying or selling bonds to banks, making it pretty easy to change the money supply as needed.[13] But in a Bitcoin-based system, the bank couldn't print money — it'd have to keep billions of dollars in Bitcoin reserves and inject or remove those reserves from the economy. The country could still change the money supply, but it would be far more limited and less flexible.

US inflation rate over time

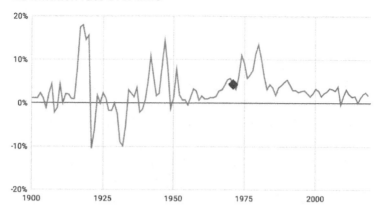

The US inflation rate, with 1971 marked with a diamond. Before that year the US was (at least partially) on the gold standard. Notice how much inflation dropped after the US adopted fiat. Source: In2013Dollars[14]

This is quite similar to the US's gold standard era. Before 1971, the government had to stockpile massive amounts of gold at Fort Knox in Kentucky to do monetary policy or trade with foreign countries.[15] And, if you've ever watched the James Bond movie *Goldfinger*, you'll know how much of a security risk it was to keep so much gold in a single spot. If the Fed had to keep massive cryptocoin reserves in some wallet, you can bet that hackers around the world would be attacking it nonstop.

But the thing that ultimately did in the gold standard was hoarding: during uncertain economic times, people tended to hoard gold, which made the government less able to get gold. With less available gold, the government couldn't inject enough money into the economy (which would have simulated it), which meant the economy would keep getting weaker. This meant that small economic troubles got magnified.[16] If the government had to use crypto, this exact thing would happen — and no government wants that.

So it doesn't make economic sense for a country to lose its ability to moderate the economy. Besides that, crypto is just impractical for running your entire economy. Remember the great Bitcoin crash of December 2017 — when the number of people wanting to trade Bitcoin peaked, transactions took hours to process and briefly cost upwards of $50.[17] If an entire country did all its financial transactions on Bitcoin, we would probably see congestion, long wait times, and high transaction prices even worse than December 2017's.

While most countries wouldn't want to abandon government-run currency in favor of cryptocurrency, countries with very weak currencies may be an exception. While cryptocurrencies are very volatile, they're better than currencies that are utterly collapsing: for instance, the Venezuelan bolivar once topped 830,000% annual inflation,[18] and the Zimbabwean dollar hit 80 billion percent annual inflation (the prices doubled every day!) back in 2008.[19] Bitcoin's occasional double-digit swings seem positively tame in comparison. So countries facing extreme currency hardship could adopt cryptocurrencies for relative stability.

Zimbabwe's infamous $100 trillion note, printed in 2008 amidst the country's massive hyperinflation. Source: Wikimedia[20]

However, if a country is already planning to abandon its currency, why not just adopt a well-established currency like the US dollar, as Zimbabwe did?[21] That would yield far greater stability than cryptocurrencies.

The verdict

In normal economic times, most citizens wouldn't want to switch from a government-backed currency to a non-governmental cryptocurrency like Bitcoin, and most national governments wouldn't want to either.

But during economic or currency collapses, though, we might start seeing cryptocurrencies being used for unofficial digital transactions. During Zimbabwe's hyperinflation crisis around 2008, for instance, people started unofficially using everything from the US dollar to the Japanese yen to the Indian rupee. But getting those currencies, both in cash and digitally, is difficult. Getting cryptocurrencies is comparatively quite easy. For all their flaws, cryptocurrencies can serve as an easy-to-access last resort for anyone, anywhere. This wasn't possible before cryptocurrencies came around, so they deserve a lot of credit for that.

In sum, while government-run currencies may become crypto-fied, we don't think they're going away anytime soon. Non-government-run cryptocurrencies will have their place in the monetary system, too, but we don't expect them to oust dollars or euros anytime soon.

The real uses of cryptocurrencies

All of this isn't to say that cryptocurrencies are worthless. They have attributes unique among currencies and thus make valuable contributions in specific areas. In our minds the two places where cryptocurrencies are the most useful: payments and investments.

Payments

As we've mentioned throughout the book, one of cryptocurrencies' unique properties is that they treat every transaction exactly the same, no matter where you're sending money, whom you're sending it to, and how much you're sending. In fact, someone once sent $300 million in Bitcoin for just 4 cents in fees![22] If you're sending small amounts of money locally, though, the transaction fees can be higher than if you'd just paid with credit card (or bank transfer, which is cheap or even free when it's allowed[23]).

And, as you know, cryptocurrencies are slow. Visa can handle about 45,000 transactions per second (*TPS*).[24] Meanwhile, Bitcoin can only handle 3 transactions per second (*TPS*),[25] and Ethereum is stuck to about 15.[26] Newer cryptocurrencies have claimed higher TPS, but troublingly, the actual TPS often falls far short of the marketed number. For instance, the Ethereum competitor EOS claims to support 4000 TPS,[27] but *TheNextWeb*'s analysis showed that it never passed 250 TPS in practice.[28]

So, while cryptocurrencies are too slow and expensive to overthrow credit cards, they have a lot of use for high-value or international payments. We think that, eventually, most remittance platforms will use stablecoins under the hood. People making larger payments will be slower to take up stablecoins because they have to be more cautious, but stablecoins will eventually be a legitimate, popular option for multi-million-dollar payments. We think that mainstream ecommerce platforms like Amazon will eventually accept stablecoins to serve people who don't use the merchant's native currency or live in another country; Facebook's emerging cryptocurrencies serve similar purposes.

According to *Tokenomics* author Thomas Power, it's not likely that a single cryptocurrency will rise above the rest for payments. Because each type of payment is different, it's more likely that we'll see six to ten specialized cryptocurrencies at the top. One cryptocurrency might focus on security and legal compliance so it can master the high-value payments space, while another might specialize in mobile banking so it can be the best for international payments

Investments

Non-stablecoins are an interesting investment option: they're very high risk and very high reward, making them better than stocks for hyper-aggressive investors.

The good news is that cryptocurrencies are slowly being accepted as investment options. You can now invest in Bitcoin for your retirement account;[29] buy Bitcoin in popular finance apps like PayPal,[30] Robinhood,[31] and Square's Cash App;[32] and buy cryptocurrency *ETFs* (*exchange-traded funds*), or aggregations of multiple cryptocurrencies in a single financial asset.[33]

Big financial players are dipping their toes in the water as well. Goldman Sachs announced in 2018 that it would be opening a Bitcoin trading division. The division wouldn't buy and sell actual bitcoins but rather "contracts linked to the price of Bitcoin;"[34] still, that's a big step forward. Even JPMorgan, whose CEO famously called Bitcoin a "fraud," announced it would start trading Bitcoin *futures*,[35] which are contracts saying a buyer will buy a certain number of items for a certain price at a certain time.[36]

This institutional exploration is making cryptocurrencies seem like more legitimate investments,[37] but cryptocurrencies still have a long way to go. According to former Nasdaq EVP John Jacobs, the biggest thing holding cryptocurrencies back is their volatility — nobody wants to put their retirement savings in something that could lose half its value in a year. Jacobs says that the key to reducing volatility isn't necessarily more or less regulation — it's sensible regulation that prevents emotions or sudden newsflashes from sending the market on a "roller coaster" trajectory.

It still isn't clear what the right set of regulations is, but Thomas Power named the replacement of ICOs with STOs as a clear step in the right direction. Many have also said that KYC and AML laws — which force exchanges to know who's buying cryptocurrencies from them, thus reducing the risk of money laundering — have "saved cryptocurrencies" by reducing their value to criminals.[38]

According to Power, the UK's Financial Conduct Authority is thinking hard about the necessary regulations to make cryptocurrencies proper investments, and he thinks that once the FCA is satisfied, the rest of the investment world will follow suit. Nasdaq is also waiting for the right regulations to fall into place; it has said that it's open to becoming a cryptocurrency exchange when the space "matures" and is properly regulated.[39]

This regulation is, on the whole, a good thing for crypto. According to Mike Novogratz, a former Goldman Sachs partner and the founder of the hedge fund Galaxy Investment Partners, more regulation will make *institutional investors* happy. Institutional investors are organizations that invest on behalf of others — think pensions, endowments, mutual funds, and hedge funds[40] — and they need cryptocurrencies to be stable and well-regulated before they can invest in them.

But, on the flip side, all the regulation makes it harder for everyday investors to get into crypto. This undermines cryptocurrencies' goal to become an investment vehicle for everyone, says Novogratz.

Once the proper regulations are in place, Jacobs expects that cryptocurrencies will supplement, not replace, stocks and bonds as the primary investment vehicles. Trading cryptocurrencies is slow and expensive compared to trading stocks and bonds, so cryptocurrencies just aren't cut out for the kinds of high-speed trading popular on Wall Street. Novogratz thinks that cryptocurrencies are a good fit for institutional investors, though, since they don't need to buy or sell assets frequently. What's more, institutional investors would appreciate cryptocurrencies' rapid growth potential for more aggressive portfolios.

In the short term, Jacobs believes that cryptocurrency ETFs are the primary way people will invest in cryptocurrencies. Since ETFs average out the performance of several cryptocurrencies, investing in an ETF means you're betting on the cryptocurrency market as a whole, not one particular cryptocurrency — a much safer bet in an era when cryptocurrencies can boom or bust overnight.

The challenge for ETF investors remains that most cryptocurrencies' prices move in tandem — when Bitcoin surges, everything else surges, and when Bitcoin plunges, everything else plunges.[41] That means that ETFs' usual selling point — that they even out the variation between individual investments, making for a smoother and more reliable investment — doesn't really work.

However, Jacobs believes that, in the long term, each cryptocurrency will have a different valuation based on the underlying payment system, blockchain, app, or other value that the currency enables — much like how stocks are priced based on the performance of the company that sells them. That is, if Jacobs's theory is right, cryptocurrencies' prices won't be so tightly correlated going forward, making them a more stable and reliable investment.

One last positive sign for crypto investors is that deep-pocketed companies are pouring huge amounts of money into cryptocurrencies, especially Bitcoin. The financial tech company Square invested $50 million into Bitcoin in 2020,[42] and the asset management company Grayscale bought tens of billions of dollars of bitcoins the same year.[43] (By 2021, Grayscale owned almost 3% of all the bitcoins in existence![44]) Even seemingly random companies have been buying Bitcoin: the business analytics firm MicroStrategy dumped billions of dollars into Bitcoin in 2020 and 2021.[45] This influx of institutional investment may help reduce Bitcoin's volatility, thus weakening one of the biggest barriers to its mass adoption as an investment.

Replacing gold

People have been comparing Bitcoin to gold for years now,[46] and while it's almost become a punchline, the comparison does merit a closer look.

One reason why gold has remained such a popular investment is that it tends to move inversely to the US dollar;[47] the price of gold (measured in dollars) usually goes up when the price of a dollar (measured in euros, yen, or a basket of other currencies) goes down, and vice versa. This happens precisely because the price of gold is measured in dollars: when a dollar gets less valuable, you need more dollars to pay for the same amount of gold, thus raising the price of gold. So, while inflation is usually a bad thing for investors, it's a good thing for gold holders.

Gold vs. the US Dollar, 2010-2020

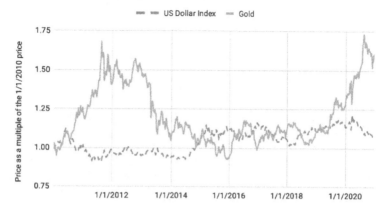

Gold has long moved inversely to the US dollar. The 2015–2019 period shows a particularly strong correlation. Source: Google Finance[4849]

In other words, gold is a useful *inflation hedge*[50]: investors often put some money into gold to safeguard against predicted inflation.

But there are signs that gold's days as the most popular inflation hedge may be numbered. Bitcoin's price also moves inversely to the US dollar, and during the COVID19 economic crisis, it became clear that Bitcoin rose along with expected inflation in the US,[51] thus making Bitcoin an inflation hedge too. Since Bitcoin's growth has blown gold's out of the water, many investors have started wondering if they should move start using Bitcoin as their inflation hedge instead of gold.[52]

It's not just the growth; Bitcoin has many other advantages over gold as an investment. For one, Bitcoin's supply is predictable; everyone knows that only 21 million coins will ever be mined. Meanwhile, nobody knows exactly how much gold is left in the Earth; estimates range from 150,000 metric tons to 2.5 million metric tons.[53] (Plus, if asteroid mining becomes commonplace, the supply of gold will become effectively infinite.) Bitcoin is also easier to store, transport, and subdivide than gold; there's no need for heavy gold bars or expensive melting and reforging.

And, perhaps most importantly, Bitcoin's algorithmic nature makes it less prone to fraud than gold. History has seen examples of people making counterfeit gold bars[54] and mining companies adding gold dust to their ore samples to trick investors into thinking that their gold mine was more lucrative than it really was.[55]

Despite these positive factors, it's unlikely that Bitcoin will totally replace gold. Bitcoin remains a poor store of value; throughout the years, it's repeatedly shed half or more of its market value within just a few hours.[56] Analysts have also argued that Bitcoin's scarcity is completely artificial; it's possible that the Bitcoin community could agree to raise the cap of 21 million bitcoins in the future.[57]

Other niches

From all of this, it's clear that the two biggest use cases for cryptocurrencies going forward will be as payment methods (primarily for large or international transfers) and as investments (supplementing, but not replacing, stocks and bonds).

Besides that, cryptocurrency retains some niche use as a way to make anonymous, private payments. An activist wanting to donate to the opposition party in a dictatorship would want their payment to remain anonymous, for instance.

The trouble is that, with each passing year, making anonymous and private cryptocurrency payments gets harder and harder. This is because most regulation, from anti-money-laundering requirements to the SEC's STO laws, has focused on tying real-world identities to crypto addresses. This is great for the crypto market as a whole because it makes cryptocurrencies less useful for criminals; one of the big things holding crypto back is the popular perception that it's only used by criminals.[58] But it means that cryptocurrencies will also become less and less useful as privacy and anonymity tools for legitimate uses, meaning that this niche of theirs will continue to shrink.

This is all deeply ironic: the reason cryptocurrencies will succeed (in terms of how much they're used) is because they're abandoning a lot of their original philosophical goals. The technology designed to upend the monetary system and cut out banks and governments is being integrated with the monetary system, adopted by banks, and regulated by governments.

Private vs. public blockchains

When you're thinking about the future of blockchains, it's helpful to look at public and private blockchains separately, since they are used for very different purposes and encounter very different challenges. (Cryptocurrencies are built on public blockchains, so new altcoins are included with public blockchains for this analysis.)

Private blockchains, at a high level, help organizations optimize the flow of information and goods through processes they control. When Walmart built a private blockchain for its leafy greens supply chain, it wanted to better understand how vegetables moved throughout its supply chain. When Xbox created a private blockchain for royalty payments, it wanted to automate the movement of money between customers, publishers, and contractors. And, thinking way back to the introduction, when the UN started tracking refugees' digital "credits" on a blockchain, it wanted to better track how many supplies each refugee could still buy. In all these cases, the organizations owned the whole process

— Walmart's supply chain, Xbox's royalty payment scheme, the UN's aid program.

Public blockchains, at a high level, aim to track the ownership and movement of assets held by the general public. Cryptocurrencies track the movement of people's money, BandNameVault tried to track trademark ownership, FileCoin tracks the "rental" of people's computer storage, and Namecoin tried to track the ownership and sale of website names. In all these cases, the blockchains' creators tried to go around centralized power brokers: cryptocurrencies want to cut out banks and governments, BandNameVault wanted to go around national trademark offices, FileCoin and IPFS want to avoid giant websites like GeoCities or MySpace, and Namecoin wanted to go around traditional domain registrars.

In short, private blockchains are process optimizations imposed from the top down, while public blockchains are radical new ways to track valuable things, grown from the bottom up. They're very different ways of using the same technology.

Different records

Private blockchains have had a relatively strong record so far. They have already transformed several sectors: supply chains, clearinghouses, and royalty payments, to name a few. And all kinds of companies can now build private blockchain apps now that Microsoft's Azure,[59] Amazon Web Services,[60] Oracle,[61] Google Cloud, IBM,[62] and other cloud computing services now offer cloud blockchain solutions.

Meanwhile, public blockchains' only major success story has been with cryptocurrencies, and even those are facing increasing scrutiny and regulation as they grow. Projects to build decentralized versions of current centralized networks, such as

IPFS's decentralized internet, are still niche projects used mostly by enthusiasts. And some of the more ambitious projects, like those to reinvent trademarks or website registration, have failed.

Different challenges

Why have public blockchains done so much worse than private blockchains? We'd say it's because public blockchains face three big kinds of challenges, but private blockchains have an easier time on all three fronts.

First, public blockchains suffer from chicken-and-egg problems. You'd only join IPFS, FileCoin, Namecoin, or other such platforms if other people were already using it, but if everyone thinks like that, nobody will join the platform. Private blockchains don't have to worry about these problems because the companies who build them can just force people to use them. If Walmart wants its vegetable suppliers to track shipments on a new blockchain, Walmart just needs to tell them to do so — any supplier who wants to keep working with Walmart will immediately comply.

Second, public blockchains have increasingly high technical complexity, making them hard to build. For instance, the ZCash cryptocurrency, launched in 2018, promises to let users make truly anonymous transactions;[63] the whitepaper detailing how ZCash works is 62 pages of dense mathematical proofs.[64] Meanwhile, private blockchains are generally less complicated; most aren't much more complex than Bitcoin or Ethereum. Plus, since most cloud providers offer blockchains-as-a-service,[65] companies that want private blockchains can rent them instead of having to build them from scratch.

The biggest, and most interesting, problem facing public blockchains is the challenge of legitimacy. Decentralized agreement over ownership only works if everyone agrees that the decentralized system is legitimate and can enforce their claims to ownership. Like BandNameVault, you can track trademarks on a blockchain, but nobody will use it unless you could back up trademark claims in court. You could track the ownership and sale of land on a blockchain, but courts wouldn't accept that as evidence and banks wouldn't accept it as collateral for a loan. (What's stopping someone from making a fake blockchain and "recording" them buying the Empire State Building?)

Meanwhile, Xbox will definitely accept its own private blockchain as legitimate — so any game publisher can be confident that Xbox will honor any payment recorded on the blockchain.

Private blockchains have it easier because they have such a limited scope. Instead of trying to reinvent how society tracks the ownership of land or art or intellectual property, they are content with upgrading the technology behind a financial clearinghouse.

Different futures

Blockchains are just tools, and as such, they shine when they have to solve technical problems like automating a supply chain. They're great for improving highly-inefficient, complex systems that are currently based on old technology or paper. But by themselves, blockchains can't reshape society in the way that many public blockchain apps hope to do — blockchains are just tools. To drive social change, the people behind public blockchains need to do the difficult "people" work of building communities, gaining media attention, and working with governments to create policies. So far, at least, startups working on public blockchains have been very excited about building the technology but less excited about doing the "people" work.

For this reason, we're more bullish on private blockchains, which don't have to deal with "people" problems — they just need to solve technical problems, and they do so admirably. Mike Novogratz and John Jacobs shared this sentiment: they believed private blockchains, despite being less sexy and ambitious than public blockchains, have more potential to change the world.

Bubble or revolution?

This is the question we set out to answer at the start of this book. As you've seen by now, the answer is more nuanced than "crypto is a bubble" or "crypto is a revolution." Blockchains, cryptocurrencies, and related technologies — that is, crypto — will change the world, not through anarchy (as many people believe) but through sheer efficiency. They'll have tremendous impact, but not in the way the creators intended.

Reversal

When Satoshi Nakamoto set out his vision for Bitcoin, he envisioned a world where currency was no longer in the control of banks and governments and people could build a financial system without having to trust any powerful institution.[66] Most cryptocurrencies since have had a similar ethos. It soon became apparent, though, that it was impractical to build an economy around decentralized, government-free money: you've read plenty about cryptocurrencies' problems with volatility, speed, price, and bandwidth. Plus, cryptocurrencies aren't always as decentralized as they look — consider how much China dominates Bitcoin.

Cryptocurrency has begun to meet with more success as it's started playing nicer with banks and governments. Stablecoins can be the foundation for a revolution in payments, but they cannot exist without strong fiat currencies. Cryptocurrency is slowly becoming a mainstream investment vehicle, but only because it's being regulated in a way that makes banks and the SEC happy. Countries are adopting cryptocurrency, but only by tokenizing their existing fiat currencies.

The future of cryptocurrencies, it seems, is not in community-run coins that replace banks and weaken governments but rather in highly-regulated coins that are smoothly integrated into the existing legal, financial, and political systems.

Blockchain has had a similar reversal. It was originally designed as a technology that could "record everything of value to humankind"[67] and lead to an era of "decentralized man" where everything — patents, copyrights, art, real estate, stocks — would be stored as crypto-tokens.[68] But a lot of the efforts to "put everything on the blockchain" we've seen so far are either stuck in prototype phase or have fallen flat. Public blockchains aren't always decentralized, either; Ethereum's founder, Vitalik Buterin, has unilaterally forced Ethereum to do a hard fork before, overriding the complaints of some in the community.[69]

Meanwhile, private blockchains are helping industries tremendously by making huge, complex processes more efficient: monitoring crops' soil temperature,[70] managing car warranties,[71] tracking airplanes' maintenance history,[72] and such. These are unsexy problems to be solving, and private blockchains aren't always perfect tools,[73] but still, private blockchains are making a real contribution to the world.

But if you look at the history of cryptocurrencies thus far, this utopic vision doesn't really work. The price of a bitcoin grew tenfold from July 2017 to December 2017 but collapsed by over 80% in the year that followed.[74] And, during the brief high, making transactions was slow, expensive, and difficult. So, as nice as the idea of decentralized, government-free money is, it's not (yet) feasible to build an economy around it.

Public blockchains are closer to what the early innovators of blockchain intended — a decentralized way to track any kind of asset. But the real success of blockchain seems to be coming from private blockchains, which are actually pretty centralized.

The ultimate irony

Thus, the ultimate irony of crypto, and perhaps the central theme of this book, is that crypto is succeeding by doing exactly the opposite of what it was originally intended for. Non-government-run cryptocurrencies like Bitcoin and public blockchains like Ethereum stay close to the founding ethos of decentralization, but it's far more likely that government-run cryptocurrencies (i.e. tokenized currencies) and private blockchains will win out. Crypto will make governments and big corporations more, and not less, powerful — consider how the blockchain helped titans like Walmart and Microsoft grow their profits, or how China can dominate more of the world's countries and economies thanks to tokenized currency.

But why this inversion? One reason is technical limitations: the massive amount of money and resources needed to create a non-volatile cryptocurrency can only really be marshaled by governments and massive corporations like Facebook, and the slowness, expense, and complexity of blockchains makes them unsuited for everyday use but doable for a dedicated company. But technology moves fast, and maybe these limitations will be solved by the next big cryptocurrency or blockchain platform.

The more fundamental, and interesting, reason comes down to the technologies' founding philosophies and theories of change.

Blockchains and cryptocurrencies are well-built technologies: they're secure and reliable, and the computational theory behind them is solid. The idea of an immutable, shared history of past transactions is extremely powerful.

But, when these technologies came out, not much serious thought was put behind the nitty gritty of how these technologies would actually drive social change. Sure, you can start tracking real estate and stocks on the blockchain, but who is going to turn those systems from prototypes into battle-hardened systems used — and accepted — by the whole world? Sure, you can make a new currency, but how would you overhaul the entire world's financial system, which is a huge and hard-to-understand beast? Sure, you can build the technology to replace governments with smart contracts and blockchain-based governance systems, but how would you get the policy, law, and statecraft right? The technologists who created blockchain and cryptocurrencies were better at solving the thorny technical problems and not these social problems.

If you created a colony on Mars and declared from the outset that all money would be cryptocurrency and all asset ownership, contracts, products, and services would use the blockchain, that might just work. The problem is that Earth is nothing like that: our economic, social, and political systems have formed over millennia. Changing them is extremely difficult and slow, and most people want a system that just works over a chaotic, untested new system. Perhaps the creators of crypto were too optimistic: you can't just "disrupt" governments that oversee millions of people, banks that handle billions of dollars, and economies that move trillions of dollars a year.

The big picture

Crypto is useful any time there's an inefficient system that needs a purely technical solution: streamlining international payments, fixing broken supply chains, and so on. But once you start getting into "people" problems — law, governance, economics, and such — crypto, like all technologies, runs into trouble.

Thus, most of the people successfully using crypto are those who just need better technical tools. These tend to be big companies, governments, and banks, who are using blockchains and cryptocurrencies to increase efficiency, transparency, security, and savings. These are all good things, but they sure aren't what the creators of crypto planned for. The technologies designed to decentralize power have turned out to give those with power even more.

So, bubble or revolution? In the short term, cryptocurrencies will definitely see their values spike and crash, and blockchain apps will come and go. But we don't think cryptocurrencies and blockchains are a bubble in the long run because they definitely have value, and they will definitely change the world — just not in the ways they were intended to.

Conclusion

THAT'S a wrap for *Bubble or Revolution*. We hope you found it informative, interesting, and maybe even fun. And we hope that you know enough to decide for yourself whether crypto is just a bubble or a bona fide revolution.

There's plenty more information in the remainder of the book, though: read on to see our glossary of the most important crypto terms (including many we didn't get to cover in the meat of the book) and 25 of the top cryptocurrencies. We also provide endnotes with links to the sources we used in our research, in case you'd like to do further research.

Want a free copy of our #1 bestselling book?

Our first book, *Swipe to Unlock*, provides a breakdown of must-know technology concepts — from cloud computing to self-driving cars — and case studies analyzing tech business strategy and technology trends. This #1 business bestseller has been featured in publications including the *Wall Street Journal*, *Forbes*, and *Business Insider*.

If you share what you liked about *Bubble or Revolution* in an Amazon review, we'll send you a free digital copy of *Swipe to Unlock* (MSRP $34.99). **Just email a screenshot of your "Verified Purchase" review for *Bubble or Revolution* to team@swipetounlock.com and we'll send you your free copy of *Swipe to Unlock*!**

Want us to speak at your company, conference, or university?

If you enjoyed *Bubble or Revolution* and want us to speak at your organization's event, email <u>speaking@bubbleorrevolution.com</u> with details about your event and the approximate dates. We always love meeting our readers in person, and we've really enjoyed the conversations we've had so far about the future of blockchains, cryptocurrencies, and the tech industry in general.

Neel Mehta, Product Manager at Google

Adi Agashe, Product Manager at Microsoft

Parth Detroja, Product Manager at Facebook

Stay in touch!

The three of us regularly share predictions of the future of the tech industry, tips for breaking into tech, and career resources on LinkedIn. You can find us and contact us at:

- linkedin.com/in/neel-a-mehta
- linkedin.com/in/adityaagashe
- linkedin.com/in/parthdetroja

Also, if you write a post about what you liked about *Bubble or Revolution* and tag us, we'll all connect with you and like, comment on, or share your post to help you get more views and followers.

Thank you again for reading, and until next time, all the best!

Acknowledgements

Writing a book takes a village, and here we'd like to thank everyone who helped make this book possible.

Neel

I remember that my parents and sister were slightly incredulous when they heard I was writing my second book. But, nonetheless, they supported me every step of the way — and their love and encouragement were invaluable.

I'd like to thank my friends Brian Lam, Brian Sapozhnikov, David Lietjauw, Jeffrey He, and Maitreyee Joshi for giving feedback on the book, critiquing the cover, and hunting down typos. I'd also like to thank Dacheng Zhao and Kush Sharma for the engaging conversations on cryptocurrencies and the future of money. You're all a big part of this book's success!

Finally, I'd like to thank the hundreds of students I've gotten to speak to about technology in the last few years. Your enthusiasm never fails to inspire me. I'd also like to thank everyone who has told me that my writings have helped them — hearing that has been one of the most rewarding things I've ever experienced. I certainly wouldn't keep writing if it weren't for you.

Adi

I would like to thank everyone who patiently helped us along the way — we wouldn't have been able to do it without your support.

First, a sincere thank you to our *Swipe to Unlock* fans — we are so grateful for your enthusiasm and genuine interest in our content!

Next, I'd like to thank all my friends who helped with everything from reviewing chapters to looking over cover designs — thanks Kei Yoshikoshi, Jimmy Xia, Sai Naidu, Winny Sun, Valerie Mack, Bowen Zhang, Hilawi Belachew, and Serguei Balanovich. Also, a huge shout-out to Li Chai, who tirelessly helped out with the design heavy lifting for the book cover, website, and other branding. And finally, thanks to my family for their support and love throughout this journey.

Parth

A huge thank you is in order for all the friends and family who helped us get this book to where it is today. I'd like to especially thank Christina Gee, Stephanie Xu, Niketan Patel, Krishna Detroja, Adam Harrison, and Kevin Cole. These kind individuals provided their valuable time, skills, opinions, and insights on everything from content to design to marketing. I am incredibly grateful for having the support of such amazing friends and family.

From all of us

We'd like to thank all the experts we got to speak to throughout our research. Your perspectives on decentralized technologies were invaluable — this book would not be the same without your guidance, wisdom, and input. Thank you Mike Novogratz, Mike Rowan, Kevin Werbach, Nathaniel Popper, John Jacobs, John Halamka, Vinny Lingham, Muneeb Ali, Arianna Simpson,

Kendrick Nguyen, Mike Jacobs, Thomas Power, Marc Mercuri, Chris Stout, Ari Juels, Bryant Nielson, Susan Athey, Maurice Herlihy, Steven Gordon, Hank Korth, Lewis Tseng, Banu Ozkazanc-Pan, and Gur Huberman.

We'd also like to thank everyone who gave us strategic advice; sourced case studies; identified people to interview about this deep, technical space; gathered feedback on our design; and helped edit chapters. It has been such a pleasure working with you, and you made this book happen. Thank you Richard Cho, Abhay Gupta, Gracie Jing, Haley Mathews, Ross Sarcona, Bani Singh, Max Hsu, Nicole Jourdain, Haimeng Gan, Kelly Chan, Andrew Granski, Sankalp Panigrahi, William Raj, Alicia Wang, Nelly Lin, Amy Huang, Siyana Popova, and John Gallagher.

And finally, we'd like to thank you, the reader! We hope you enjoyed reading *Bubble or Revolution* as much as we enjoyed writing it.

|

Appendix A.
Number Systems

We humans are used to counting in base-10, or decimal: we have ten digits and build numbers by using ones, tens, hundreds, and thousands places (and so on). When you see "327" written down somewhere, your head is calculating $(3 * 10^2) + (2 * 10^1) + (7 * 10^0)$ $= 300 + 20 + 7 = 327$. We're so used to base-10 that we often forget that it's just another way of counting.

Binary

Computers, for instance, don't think in base-10. In fact, they only understand the numbers 0 and 1, making their number system base-2, or *binary*. (Why just 0 and 1? Computers rely on electrical signals that can be either on [1] or off [0] at any given time.[1])

This means that, instead of ones, tens, and hundreds places, computers use ones, two, fours, and eights places (and so on). Each place in a binary number can only contain a 0 or 1; after 1, you have to jump up a place. To count from zero to ten in binary, you'd count 0, 1, 10, 11, 100, 101, 110, 111, 1000, 1001, 1010. Each time you add 1 to a 1, it rolls back to 0 and carries a 1 forward to the place to its left. It's just like how we humans, when learning how to add in elementary school, knew to "carry the 1" when we added two digits that summed to more than ten.

Binary numbers can be broken down just like decimal numbers: the number 10101 in binary computes to $(1 * 2^4) + (0 * 2^3) + (1 * 2^2) + (0 * 2^1) + (1 * 2^0) = 16 + 0 + 4 + 0 + 1 = 21$ in decimal.

Binary is great for computers under the hood, but it's not very efficient to write down. Numbers written in binary take about three times as many digits as numbers written in decimal.[a] The number 1776 in decimal (four digits) is 11011110000 in binary (eleven digits).

Hexadecimal

So technologists often turn to a system called base-16, or hexadecimal, to more compactly write numbers used by computers. Hexadecimal crams four digits of binary information into a single digit (since $16 = 2^4$), making it a very efficient way to write down numbers used by computers.

Instead of 0 and 1 or 0-9, base-16 uses 0-9 plus the letters A-F (that's sixteen possible digits). If you were counting from zero to twenty in hexadecimal, you'd count 0, 1, 2, 3, 4, 5, 6, 7, 8, 9, A, B, C, D, E, F, 10, 11, 12, 13, 14. That's right, A is our ten and F is our fifteen.

(Are the mishmash of number systems confusing you yet? Fortunately, there's a way out: because hexadecimal often looks a lot like decimal, technologists often put the tag "0x" at the front of a hexadecimal number.)

---

[a] The exact multiple is $\log(10)/\log(2) = 3.32$.

Like binary numbers, hexadecimal numbers can be easily converted to decimal. 0xB5D is $(11 * 16^2) + (5 * 16^1) + (13 * 16^0)$ = 2816 + 80 + 13 = 2909 in decimal. 0x53 is $(5 * 16^1) + (3 * 16^0)$ = 80 + 3 = 83 in decimal. (This is where the 0x tag really comes in handy.)

Hexadecimal is even more compact than decimal, since hexadecimal uses even more digits. For instance, remember how 1776 is four digits in decimal and eleven digits in binary. In hexadecimal, it's represented as 0x6F0 — just three digits!

Decimal	Binary	Hexadecimal
0	0	0
1	1	1
2	10	2
3	11	3
4	100	4
5	101	5
6	110	6
7	111	7
8	1000	8
9	1001	9
10	1010	A
11	1011	B
12	1100	C
13	1101	D
14	1110	E
15	1111	F
16	10000	10

Hexadecimal is everywhere when you start peering under the hood of your apps and gadgets. Computer error codes[2] and video game cheat codes[3] are often written in hexadecimal (or just "hex," in techie jargon.) If you open an image file in a text editor, you'll see hex.[4]

And, of course, Bitcoin loves hexadecimal, especially for hashes: Bitcoin uses hex to encode block hashes[5] and transaction hashes.[6]

```
A problem has been detected and windows has been shut down to prevent damage
to your computer.

The problem seems to be caused by the following file: SPCMDCON.SYS

PAGE_FAULT_IN_NONPAGED_AREA

If this is the first time you've seen this Stop error screen,
restart your computer. If this screen appears again, follow
these steps:

Check to make sure any new hardware or software is properly installed.
If this is a new installation, ask your hardware or software manufacturer
for any windows updates you might need.

If problems continue, disable or remove any newly installed hardware
or software. Disable BIOS memory options such as caching or shadowing.
If you need to use Safe Mode to remove or disable components, restart
your computer, press F8 to select Advanced Startup Options, and then
select Safe Mode.

Technical information:

*** STOP: 0x00000050 (0xFD3094C2,0x00000001,0xFBFE7617,0x00000000)

*** SPCMDCON.SYS - Address FBFE7617 base at FBFE5000, DateStamp 3d6dd67c
```

One of Windows's infamous "blue screens of death," shown when your computer crashes. At the bottom you see hexadecimal error codes. Source: Wikimedia[7]

Bitcoin's bases

For an extra-compact representation of a number, you can use base-64, which uses 64 digits: the 10 Arabic numerals, the 26 uppercase letters, the 26 lowercase letters, and the special characters "+" and "/".[8]

The problem with base-64 is that it's not very human-readable. It uses several symbols that are easy to confuse: lowercase "o," uppercase "O," and the numeral 0, and lowercase "l" (as in "llama"), uppercase "I" (as in "India"), and the numeral 1. So if you were trying to, say, type in a base-64 number that you were reading off a piece of paper, you'd have a good chance of getting it wrong. Some niche problems affect "+" and "/"; for instance, some text fields don't accept non-alphanumeric characters.[9]

Satoshi developed the base-58 number system to solve these problems. It includes all the base-64 digits minus "+," "/," uppercase "O," the numeral 0, uppercase "I" (as in "India"), and lowercase "l" (as in "llama"). This leaves 58 possible digits, which is still plenty to compactly represent a number.[b] Bitcoin uses base-58 quite often; it's the standard format for private keys, public keys, and addresses.[10]

This paper wallet contains a private key and address written in base-58.[11]

---

[b] Base-64 is 50% more compact than hexadecimal: $\log(64)/\log(16)$ = 1.5. Base-58 is 46% more compact than hexadecimal: $\log(58)/\log(16)$ = 1.46. Base-58's greater usability makes up for its tiny loss in compactness.

Appendix B.
Macroeconomics

We've all heard of supply and demand, and you've probably read about how reducing supply and increasing demand drives up the prices of goods. That kind analysis — of individual goods and companies — is called *microeconomics*.

The other half of economics is *macroeconomics*, the study of large-scale economies. Whenever you hear talk about inflation, the Fed, monetary policy, exchange rates, unemployment, and other "big-picture" concepts, that's macroeconomics. Because cryptocurrencies have their own multi-billion-dollar economies attached to them, macroeconomics is a key tool in understanding how these currencies work.

Real and nominal

The first thing you have to know about macroeconomics — the study of the economy as a whole — is the difference between *real* and *nominal* quantities. *Nominal* quantities refer to an amount of money, while *real* quantities refer to an amount of "stuff," like the amount of goods and services you can buy.[1]

For instance, if you go to a burger joint, the amount of money you have in your pocket is a nominal quantity, while the number of burgers you can buy with that money is a real quantity. Real quantities matter more: what'll make you happy is not the amount of money you spend but rather the number of burgers you get. (Having $100 in your pocket wouldn't be of much use if every burger cost $100; in other words, nominal quantities aren't what really matter to people.)

Many other economic quantities are measured in terms of real vs. nominal. The nominal interest rate of a loan or credit card, for instance, is the percent you see on the contract, but the real interest rate would account for inflation.[2] The nominal rate of return of a stock is the raw percent that the stock price grew from last year to this year,[3] while the real rate of return takes inflation into account and tells you how much more stuff you could buy if you sold that stock this year instead of last year.[4]

For instance, if a stock's price nominally grew by 10% in a year but inflation was 2%, the real return was only 8% — meaning you could only buy 8% more shoes, airline tickets, and so on with those earnings.

In short, money is nominal while "stuff" — sandwiches, haircuts, etc. — is real.

Money

What is "money," anyway? Economists' standard answer to that question is that money serves three purposes:

- It's a medium of exchange; you can use it for all transactions.

- It's a unit of account; you can measure your wealth with a single number.
- It's a store of value; it'll remain valuable for a long period of time.[5]

US dollars and other fiat currencies fulfill all three purposes. Cattle fail this test: not everyone wants to be paid in cows, it's hard to measure the value of other things in terms of cows (each cow has a different value, anyway), and cows become much less valuable when they die or get eaten.

Cryptocurrencies are clearly media of exchange and units of account; you should (in theory) be able to buy anything with them, and you can (again, in theory) measure the value of anything with them. The big question is if they are stores of value;[6] cryptocurrencies' volatility would make many people hesitant to store all their wealth in cryptocoins.

Inflation

Imagine an economy where everyone bought everything with one-dollar bills. In this world, a total of Y goods and services[a] are bought every year, and the average price of each good/service is P. That means the total amount of money spent in the economy — the economy's output — each year is PY. (PY is also known as the *nominal GDP,*, while Y — which ignores money and focuses on "stuff" — is known as the *real GDP*. P is known as the *price level*.)[7]

---

[a] Measured in terms of some real quantity; usually inflation-adjusted dollars.

The amount of dollar bills in the economy is known as the money supply, M.[8b] Each dollar bill can be spent one or more times each year; the average number of times a bill changes hands in a year is the *money velocity*, or V.[9] (If you pay a dollar bill to a bakery in January, the bakery's owner spends it in a supermarket in August, and the supermarket pays an employee with it in December, that bill changed hands three times in a year, so its velocity is 3. V is the average velocity of all bills.) So, the total number of dollars spent in the economy is MV.

That means that MV and PY both express the amount of money spent each year. So we can say that:

$$MV = PY.$$

This is known as the *quantity theory of money*,[10] and it's used to analyze inflation.

---

[b] Macroeconomists define different levels of money. In decreasing order of liquidity, they are C or M0 (cash), M1 (cash and checking accounts), and M2 (M1 plus savings accounts). Economists usually use M1 when talking about money supply.

M, V, P, and Y in the United States

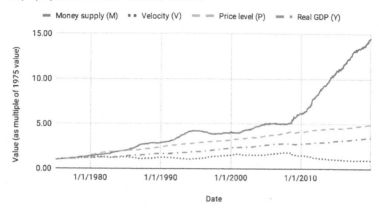

M has grown rapidly in the United States since 2010, while P and Y have been growing steadily since 1975 and V has fluctuated slightly. Data source: Federal Reserve Bank of St. Louis[11]

Testing the quantity theory of money

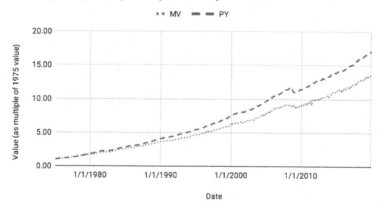

The quantity theory of money holds up pretty well: MV and PY have moved almost in lockstep, though they've slowly diverged. Data source: Federal Reserve Bank of St. Louis[12]

Changes

Suppose each quantity changes after a year, and the change in each quantity is labeled with the Greek letter Δ (delta). If the money supply changed from $1 million to $1.5 million, ΔM would be $500,000. A mathematical rule[c] lets us rewrite the quantity theory of money like this:

$$\%\Delta M + \%\Delta V = \%\Delta P + \%\Delta Y.$$

$\%\Delta M$ is the percent change in the money supply, $\%\Delta V$ is the percent change in money velocity, $\%\Delta P$ is the percent change in price level (this is inflation), and $\%\Delta Y$ is the percent change in the amount of goods and services sold (this is the real GDP growth). So the way you can measure inflation is:

$$\%\Delta P = \%\Delta M + \%\Delta V - \%\Delta Y.$$

Economists usually assume that the velocity of money is constant since it's tied to people's behavior and the structure of the economy, and those things don't change quickly.[13] So, with this assumption, $\%\Delta V = 0$, so:

$$\%\Delta P = \%\Delta M - \%\Delta Y.$$

In other words, inflation is the rate of growth in money supply minus the rate of growth of real GDP. Or, more succinctly, inflation happens when the money supply grows faster than the economy's output. So, when the central bank (or the Bitcoin software) creates more money, that doesn't always lead to inflation — inflation only happens if they make money faster than the

---

[c] Specifically, the percentage change in XY is the percentage change in X plus the percentage change in Y. Or, mathematically, $\%\Delta XY = \%\Delta X + \%\Delta Y$.

economy grows. As the economist Milton Friedman put it, inflation happens when there's "too much money chasing too few goods."[14]

Controversy

This theory is probably enough for the purposes of this book and our analyses of Bitcoin, but it's worth calling out that the theory isn't as clean as it seems. One source of controversy among economists is whether changing the amount of money in the economy (M) can affect the real output of the economy (Y). One school of thought, *monetarism*, says that money supply has no effect on real GDP.[15] In this thought, $\%\Delta Y$ would be zero, so any growth in money supply would always lead to inflation:

$$\%\Delta P = \%\Delta M.$$

Friedman, a prominent monetarist, used this thought experiment: if a helicopter dropped millions of dollar bills on a city, everyone would have more money but price levels would rise accordingly; nobody would really be able to afford more (Y wouldn't change), but there would be rampant inflation.

The problem with that argument, of course, is that central banks don't drop money out of helicopters, so other economists believe that the monetarists are wrong and that it's not as simple as "money growth leads to inflation."[16] Other economic models say that increasing the money supply actually *does* temporarily increase real GDP because it gives consumers more dollars to spend, which stimulates the economy.[17] This is why central banks like the US Federal Reserve (or the Fed) can adjust the money supply, using tools of *monetary policy*, to speed up or slow down the economy as needed.[18]

Another twist is that the monetary velocity (V) can, and does, change. During recessions, people stop spending money, so velocity decreases — this happened during the Great Depression and Great Recession.[19] Interestingly, the velocity kept dropping through the 2010s, even after the Great Recession was over, because the money supply grew ($\%\Delta M$) faster than inflation ($\%\Delta P$) and real GDP growth ($\%\Delta Y$) put together.[20] After all, if we rearrange our quantity theory equation, we get:

$$\%\Delta V = \%\Delta P + \%\Delta Y - \%\Delta M$$

Money velocity in the United States over time

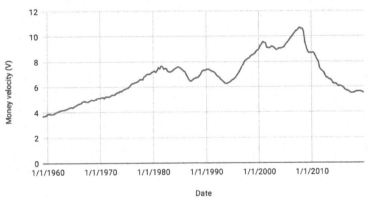

Money velocity isn't constant, but it doesn't consistently grow the way that M, P, and Y do either. Data source: Federal Reserve Bank of St. Louis[21]

Money supply and demand

As you saw (or will see) in the body of the book, money supply is relatively easy to understand, especially for Bitcoin, where coins are mined at a predictable rate. It's a bit more complicated for national economies, but roughly, a central bank like the Fed can buy or sell bonds to banks, thus adding or removing money from the economy, or change the interest rate it charges other banks (known as the *discount rate*), thus encouraging banks to borrow more or less money from the central bank.[22]

Money demand is harder to understand. The term itself seems silly: who wouldn't want to have more money? A better way to think about money demand is this: how much of your wealth would you like to keep as money (cash or checking accounts) instead of as investments (like stocks, bonds, and Bitcoin)?[23] How much do you demand money instead of investments?

Money demand boils down to tradeoffs. To think about these tradeoffs, it's useful to think about how easy it is to spend, or *liquidate*, assets. This property is known as *liquidity*, and different assets have different amounts of liquidity. Cash is the most *liquid* of all assets: you can spend it anywhere instantly. Checking accounts are a little less liquid; you'd have to go to an ATM to withdraw cash before you could spend it, but it's still pretty fast to spend money online from your checking account.

Savings accounts are less liquid still: you can only make a limited number of transfers out each month,[24] making them bad places to get spending money. Stocks, bonds, and bitcoins are even less liquid, since the only way to get cash out of them is to sell them, and completing a sale might take a few hours. Houses are among the least liquid of all assets: the primary way to get spending money out of a house is to sell it,[d] which is a big hassle.

More liquid assets pay you less interest or returns, while less liquid assets are more profitable to hold; stocks yield more returns than

---

[d] You could do a reverse mortgage if you wanted to, but reverse mortgages are best discussed in ads on the Golf Channel and not books like this.

bonds, which yield more returns than cash.[e][25] What's more, bonds that take longer to pay out (and thus are less liquid) generally offer a higher interest rate:[26]

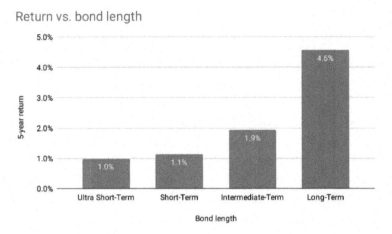

Return vs. bond length

Bonds that take longer to pay out are less liquid and generally yield higher returns. Data source: TheBalance[27]

This is for a reason: liquidity is convenient, and investors would only give up that convenience if they got some money in exchange. This is known as *liquidity preference theory*.[28] Liquidity is good, and the more liquidity you give up, the more money you expect.

With this definition, we can reformulate money demand like so: money demand is how much people want to hold liquid assets.

Two things drive money demand under this view. First is the real GDP (Y); when there's more stuff to buy, people will want to hold more cash to buy it all.[29]

---

[e] Another reason for the difference in returns is risk: higher-risk assets like stocks yield higher rewards.

Second is the *real interest rate* on bonds, which is how much a bond pays you each year, minus inflation.[30] When the interest rate goes up, it becomes more attractive to hold bonds (which are the most reliable investment), so people want to hold cash less; when the interest rate goes down, people feel less need to hold bonds and are happy to hold cash.[31] (This is an example of *opportunity cost*: the real interest rate is the opportunity cost of holding cash, since every dollar bill you hold is one less dollar you could have earned interest on. When the real interest rate goes down, the opportunity cost of holding cash goes down.)

So what does this all mean for Bitcoin? Bitcoin is an investment along with stocks and bonds, so the concept of "money demand" (which usually applies to "normal" currencies like dollars) doesn't really fit.

But we can still learn from liquidity preference theory, which says that people will want to hold cash more when the returns on less-liquid assets (like the real interest rates of bonds) decrease. First, and most obviously, investors will flock to Bitcoin when its expected returns are higher than those of other illiquid assets. Second, Bitcoin will never replace cash unless it becomes fully liquid. Third, investors will only invest in a cryptocurrency if it shows substantial gains. This hasn't been a problem for Bitcoin, which has shown plenty of growth, but it means that any cryptocurrency with low or zero returns (like the stablecoins we discuss in this book) will have trouble attracting investors.[f]

---

[f] People may still want to hold stablecoins as a sort of "checking account" for crypto funds: you can store money there safely without going through the hassle of cashing out.

Appendix C.
Who is Satoshi?

Satoshi Nakamoto, the pseudonymous creator of Bitcoin, has never publicly announced his (or her, or their, etc.) real identity. Nobody knows who Satoshi is. In fact, we don't even know if Satoshi was one person or a group of people.[1][2]

All we have from Satoshi (who is usually referred to by his first name) is a few hundred forum posts,[3] a handful of emails on public lists,[4] and a smattering of private communications with other early Bitcoin developers.[5] But that hasn't stopped Bitcoin enthusiasts from trying to figure out his life, his political and philosophical leanings, and, of course, who he really is.

The timeline

Satoshi first emerged on Halloween 2008, when he published the Bitcoin whitepaper[6][a] on a public cryptography-focused mailing list.[7] He debated and sharpened his ideas on that list throughout 2008[8] and released the first version of the Bitcoin software in

---

[a] We must say that the Bitcoin whitepaper is one of the best-written pieces of technical writing we've ever read. It explains Bitcoin better than most people ever could, and in just 8 pages to boot.

January 2009.[9] The next month, he started posting about Bitcoin on the P2P Forum, a haven for proponents of decentralized technology.[10]

Satoshi worked consistently on Bitcoin through 2009 and 2010, releasing new versions of the software and frequently engaging with people on the forums and mailing lists.[11]

His final public communication, in December 2010, was simple and unglamorous: he announced a minor update to the Bitcoin software that added some protection from *denial-of-service (DoS)* attacks, where an attacker could flood a system with spam messages and leave it unable to work for legitimate users.[12]

The public never heard from Satoshi again, but apparently Satoshi kept in touch with other Bitcoin developers for another year. Mike Hearn published the final email Satoshi wrote to him, dated April 23, 2011:

> *I've moved on to other things. It's in good hands with Gavin [Andresen, another early Bitcoin developer] and everyone.*[13]

Satoshi's final known correspondence with anyone was on April 26, 2011, when he wrote this to Andresen:

> *I wish you wouldn't keep talking about me as a mysterious shadowy figure, the press just turns that into a pirate currency angle. Maybe instead make it about the open source project and give more credit to your dev contributors; it helps motivate them.*[14]

Andresen replied to the email saying that Nakamoto had been invited to speak at an event hosted by the CIA, but Satoshi never wrote back.[15] Some conspiracy theorists believe that Satoshi was spooked by mention of the CIA[16] and, apparently, fled to avoid contact with them.

Gavin Andresen, an early Bitcoin developer and the last person known to have spoken with Satoshi. Source: Web Summit[17]

In 2015, four years after Satoshi's last known communication, someone using his email address posted about a dispute going on in the Bitcoin world around Bitcoin XT,[18] a competitor to the Bitcoin Core client software that runs on the vast majority of Bitcoin full nodes.[19]

This person, claiming to be Satoshi, said that he had come out of retirement to warn the world about this "very dangerous fork" and the developers of "this pretender-Bitcoin."[20] Bitcoin XT was created by Mike Hearn,[21] the same Bitcoin developer who had had one of the last-known communications with Satoshi, and a controversial figure in the Bitcoin community.[22]

Most experts believe that this 2015 email was not sent by Satoshi but rather by someone who had hacked Satoshi's account.[23] Why would the creator of Bitcoin have lain low for so many years, only to reemerge to join the debate over what ultimately was a minor squabble in the Bitcoin community — and promptly disappear again? And why would someone who was quite diplomatic in his communications, even with his harshest critics,[24] have so crudely attacked his former ally?

Satoshi's philosophy

So it's clear that Satoshi vanished after 2011. But ever since, Bitcoin proponents have been reading every scrap of his writings to understand his political and philosophical views, either to justify their proposals for the future of Bitcoin or just to understand the origins of the technology they love so much. There's even a book, titled *The Book of Satoshi*, that catalogs all his known writings.[25] (It's somewhat reminiscent of a religious movement trying to understand the mindset of their prophet.)

Any study of Satoshi's political opinions and the reasons he created Bitcoin must start with the cryptic message he encoded in the very first Bitcoin block ever added to the blockchain, known as the *genesis block*. The message was:

> *The Times 03/Jan/2009 Chancellor on brink of second bailout for banks.[26]*

The message referenced an article in the British newspaper *The Times*,[27] which mentioned that the Chancellor of the Exchequer (the head of the UK's treasury[28]) was considering pumping taxpayer money into failing British banks amidst the heights of the 2008 financial crisis.

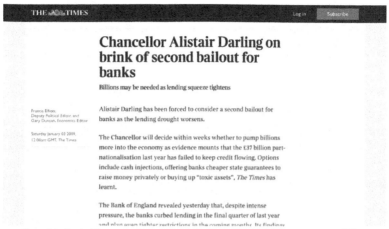

Satoshi cited this now-famous article from the British newspaper The Times *in the first Bitcoin block, which may give clues about why he created Bitcoin.*[29]

Bitcoin analysts have interpreted this to mean that Satoshi distrusted the banking system and was angry that citizens were paying for banks' mistakes. Thus, the thinking goes, Satoshi created a currency that no bank or government could control — no taxes, no bank failures, no bailouts.[30]

Satoshi's disdain for banks was made even clearer in the 2009 post where he introduced Bitcoin to the P2P Forum:

> *The root problem with conventional currency is all the trust that's required to make it work. The central bank must be trusted not to debase the currency, but the history of fiat currencies is full of breaches of that trust. Banks must be trusted to hold our money and transfer it electronically, but they lend it out in waves of credit bubbles with barely a fraction in reserve. We have to trust them with our privacy, trust them not to let identity thieves drain our accounts.*[31]

Throughout Satoshi's writings, this distrust of financial institutions is the most consistent theme. It seems that this is the main reason he created Bitcoin.

Some of Satoshi's other writings show he had a vaguely libertarian mindset. In his posts, he expressed skepticism in government authority and said he sought to "gain a new territory of freedom" with Bitcoin.[32]

But Satoshi was probably not an ideologue; it's more likely that he just created a technology he was passionate about and was happy to see that a particular community had been drawn to his creation. Just consider this quote of his:

> *It's very attractive to the libertarian viewpoint if we can explain it properly. I'm better with code than with words though.*[33]

Satoshi's identity

The ultimate question is: who is (or was) Satoshi, anyway?

One leading theory is that Satoshi is an alias for Wei Dai[34] or Nick Szabo,[35] computer scientists who made proto-cryptocurrencies (B-Money[36] and Bit Gold,[37] respectively) that predated Bitcoin but never took off. The evidence in favor of Szabo is relatively strong:

- One linguistic researcher found striking similarities between Szabo and Satoshi's writing styles, claiming that "only 0.1% of cryptography researchers could have produced this writing style."[38] Both writers used relatively rare phrases like "trusted third party," "for our purposes," and "it should be noted" quite often.[39]

- Szabo had been looking for collaborators on Bit Gold shortly before Satoshi announced Bitcoin; after the announcement, Szabo stopped writing about Bit Gold.[40]
- Satoshi referenced many ideas from Bit Gold, including proof-of-work, timestamping transactions, and the need to remove trusted third parties,[41] but he never cited Szabo's work.[42]

We asked Nathaniel Popper, the author of the Bitcoin history book *Digital Gold*, and he said that he thought Szabo was Satoshi. But all this evidence is just circumstantial, and Szabo has repeatedly denied that he is Satoshi.[43]

The British hypothesis

One theory that's more credible, in our minds, is that Satoshi is really British, and not Japanese, as is commonly believed.[b] His writings are all in perfect English, for one.[44] His original Bitcoin paper was full of British spellings (like "favour" instead of "favor"[45]), and his forum posts were full of Britishisms too ("bloody hard"[46]). He rarely posted on forums between midnight and 6am GMT,[47] which is the middle of the day in Japan but nighttime in the UK. And, finally, he cited the British paper *The Times* in the genesis block. This is indeed circumstantial evidence, but faking your own sleep schedules and native dialect isn't very easy to do.

This British evidence would lay to rest the theory that Szabo is Satoshi, since Szabo is American. Dai[48] is American as well, as was Hal Finney,[49] a computer scientist who received the first Bitcoin transaction from Satoshi and was widely rumored to be Satoshi himself.[50] The only notable Brit who Satoshi was closely associated

---

[b] He could still be Japanese-British. That is, he or his ancestors could have been born in Japan but moved to the United Kingdom.

with is Adam Back, the inventor of Hashcash, the proof-of-work algorithm that Bitcoin used.[51] Back says he was the first person Satoshi told about Bitcoin, but he denies that he is Satoshi.[52]

Another common, but widely doubted, claim is that the Australian computer scientist and businessman Craig Wright is Satoshi.[53] In one Medium post, Wright wrote:

> *Bitcoin started because of my ideas. It was my design, and it is my creation. And, making certain that it cannot be subverted by criminals is and remains my duty. I was Satoshi.[54]*

Many media outlets believed him at first,[55] but proof quickly came out that Wright was a hoaxer. The encryption keys he had used to prove that he was Satoshi were faked, several of his credentials (including his PhD) were faked, and details about his companies were fake. Even some blog posts where he had apparently been writing about Bitcoin a few days after the whitepaper came out were fake; Wright had edited them after 2013 to add the Bitcoin claims.[56] Wright refused to provide any further "proof" that he was Satoshi.[57]

Stranger claims

But, despite all these theories, nobody has conclusively proven that they are Satoshi. The lack of clarity around Satoshi's identity has led to some truly bizarre claims about him. The eccentric cybersecurity entrepreneur John McAfee (inventor of the McAfee antivirus software) claimed he had met Satoshi and threatened to expose him but quickly called off the plan; most people think McAfee was just blustering.[58]

(It's hard to overstate how weird McAfee is: he says he disguised himself as a drunk German and a Guatemalan street vendor while in exile in Belize,[59] planned to hire hundreds of people to wear masks of his face and campaign for his 2020 Presidential run because he was hiding from the IRS,[60] and claims he keeps his gun in his hand even while in the shower.[61])

The eccentric millionaire John McAfee, who claimed he could unmask Satoshi. Source: Wikimedia[62]

An even more bizarre claim was from a Pakistani man who claimed to be Satoshi.[63] He said that the name Bitcoin was from "Bank of Credit and Commerce International,"[64] a Pakistani bank that *Time* magazine once called "a financial supermarket for crooks and spies" and dubbed the sleaziest bank of all time.[65] (Quite some competition in that category.)

We could keep going, but you get the point. As long as there is Bitcoin, there will be a fascinating cottage industry of scientists (and crazies) claiming to be Satoshi and an army of digital sleuths trying to prove them right or wrong. One thing's for sure: whoever Satoshi was, his little whitepaper had a bigger impact than he probably ever could have believed.

Glossary

T HE WORLD of blockchains and cryptocurrencies has a dizzying amount of jargon. We've covered a lot of it throughout *Bubble or Revolution*, but here we'll summarize some key crypto terms, including several we didn't get room to discuss in depth during the main content of the book. And we'll also give overviews of the best-known and most important cryptocurrencies.

Terms

In this section we'll cover some of the more common buzzwords and key terms you'll hear as you read about blockchains and cryptocurrencies.

51% attack

Can occur when a miner or group of miners controls more computing power than every other miner of a particular cryptocurrency put together. (In other words, this miner or group of miners controls at least 51% of all computing power on the network.) In a 51% attack, the dominant miner or group can rewrite the blockchain at will, allowing them to award themselves unlimited amounts of money, cancel past transactions, and so on.[1]

Address

A public pseudonym for a cryptocurrency user. You need to know someone's address to send them coins.

AML

Anti-money laundering. Refers to laws and regulations placed on cryptocurrency exchanges to prevent people from using these exchanges to launder money.[2] *See also KYC.*

Archival node

A type of full node that includes not just the entire blockchain but also historical snapshots of the cryptocurrency, such as how many coins each address had at any point in time.[3] Full nodes are compressed versions of archival nodes; all the information is still there, but it's hard to do advanced calculations and queries unless you expand the full node into an archival node.[4]

ASIC

A specialized computer chip that is hyper-optimized to run a particular mining algorithm. Serious Bitcoin miners need to use ASICs, since general-purpose computers (like a MacBook) just aren't optimized enough to run the mining algorithm quickly.[5] Stands for *application-specific integrated circuit.*

ASIC-resistance

A feature of a mining algorithm, such as Ethereum's, that gives ASICs no edge over general-purpose computers. Normal mining algorithms make miners run the exact same computation over and over; miners then make ASICs that are extremely good at that computation. But ASIC-resistant mining algorithms make miners do a wide variety of computations, so a general-purpose computer (which is used to doing varied computations) performs better than any specialized chip. As Ethereum puts it, "an Ethereum ASIC would essentially be an ASIC for general computation — i.e. a better CPU."[6] ASIC-resistance is desirable because it makes mining more accessible to individuals and hobbyists.

Asset

Any resource with economic value. There are plenty of financial assets: dollars, shares of stock, cryptocurrencies, bonds, etc. But plenty of other things are assets: cars, books, property deeds, intellectual property, trademarks, etc.[7] Blockchains offer a decentralized way to track the movement of any asset.

Base-58

The format used for Bitcoin addresses. It includes uppercase letters, lowercase letters, and numbers, but removes the easily-misinterpreted characters zero, capital I, capital O, and lowercase l.[8]

Binance

A popular cryptocurrency exchange.

bitcoin (lowercase)

Refers to the units of Bitcoin currency. For instance, "Her fortune includes dozens of bitcoins." Compare this to "my friends invest in Bitcoin."

Bitcoin Core

The official version of the Bitcoin software. It includes a wallet, software for full nodes, and a transaction validation engine.[9]

Bitcoin's scaling problem

The well-known issue that Bitcoin can only support 7 transactions per second, while mainstream payment systems like Visa can support tens of thousands.[10] Congestion happens whenever Bitcoin users want to make more than 7 transactions per second; this leads to long waiting times and high transaction fees.[11]

Bitfinex

A popular cryptocurrency exchange.

Block

A bundle of cryptocurrency transactions. Miners compete to create blocks; the winning miner gets to add the block to the end of the blockchain and gets a few coins as a reward.

Blockchain

A decentralized ledger that stores an immutable history of past transactions. Cryptocurrencies are all built around a blockchain, but you can track the movement of *any* asset, digital or physical, on a blockchain. "Putting something on a blockchain" just means tracking its movement using a blockchain.

Block explorer

A tool that lets you see information about blocks, addresses, and transactions on a blockchain.[12] Notably, block explorers let you see anyone's past transactions, trading partners, and current balance if you know their address.

Block height

The total number of blocks in the blockchain.

Block reward

The number of cryptocoins that a miner gets for successfully mining a block. In several cryptocurrencies, including Bitcoin, the block reward gets cut in half every few years.[13]

Block size

The maximum file size of a block (such as 1 megabyte), which determines how many transactions can fit in a block. Since blocks get mined at constant intervals, the block size is one of the factors that determines the number of transactions per second that the cryptocurrency supports.[14]

Block time

The time taken for each block to be mined. In Bitcoin, for instance, one block is mined every 10 minutes, on average.[15]

Bubble

When the price of an asset (cryptocurrency, tulip, house, etc.) rises above its true value. Bubbles usually happen when speculation goes out of control and people keep buying the asset at an overly-high price, hoping that the price will keep going up. Bubbles inevitably burst when the speculation cycle breaks down.

Centralization

When everything in a network flows through a single entity. For instance, shopping at Walmart is centralized; goods flow from manufacturers to Walmart and then from Walmart to consumers. Compare this to a farmer's market, where goods go from farmers straight to consumers. Shopping at a farmer's market, then, is decentralized.

Client-server model

A centralized way to set up a computer network, where everyone talks to a central authority (the server). Twitter uses a client-server model: Twitter users (clients) send messages to Twitter (the server) and also fetch messages from Twitter. As an analogy, it's like sending a letter through the mail (the postal service is the server) instead of hand-delivering it (where there's no central authority). *See also peer-to-peer.*

Coinbase

A popular cryptocurrency exchange.

CoinHive

An infamous startup that offered cryptojacking code to hackers and unscrupulous website owners. This code made website visitors' computers spend all their energy mining Monero for whoever installed the code. CoinHive's software was a favorite among cybercriminals[16] until it collapsed in 2019.[17]

Cold storage

Storing the private key to your cryptocurrency "account" in something not connected to the internet. Writing your private key on a sticky note, saving it on a non-internet-connected computer, or using a hardware wallet are all forms of cold storage. This way, a hacker can't get your private key even if they get complete control over all your internet-connected devices.[18] *See also hot storage.*

CPU

A digital device's central processing unit, which does most of the device's computation, from crunching numbers in Excel to streaming movies on Netflix. Every computer has a CPUs, and CPUs can mine cryptocurrency, but they're relatively weak; a cryptocurrency that can be mined on CPUs is very friendly to beginners, who might not have any more specialized hardware.[19] *See also GPU and ASIC.*

Crowdfunding

Raising money for a venture from many small donors over the internet. ICOs are a form of crowdfunding.

Crypto

An umbrella term for the field of blockchains and cryptocurrencies.

Cryptocoin

A unit of cryptocurrency, such as a bitcoin or ether. Often lowercase. Not to be confused with the cryptocurrencies themselves, which have capitalized names like Bitcoin and Ethereum.

Cryptocurrency

A digital currency that uses a blockchain to track payments. Cryptocurrencies use cryptography to verify transactions and prevent tampering and counterfeiting, hence the "crypto" prefix.

Cryptography

The science of encoding information in a way that's hard to reverse-engineer. In cryptocurrency, cryptography is used for proving your identity ("logging in"), preventing tampering with past transactions on the blockchain, making mining hard, and other crucial features.[20]

Cryptojacking

The unauthorized use of your device to mine cryptocurrency for someone else. This often happens when hackers install mining code on a hacked website; if you visit the site, your browser app will run that code and mine cryptocoins (usually Monero) that go to the hacker's wallet. Some unscrupulous website owners install this mining code on their own sites as a way to make money off unsuspecting visitors.[21] If you get cryptojacked, none of your money is stolen, but your CPU spends all its energy mining, which drains your battery and makes your device overheat and slow to a crawl.[22]

DAO

A decentralized autonomous organization; refers to a service or company that runs off nothing but smart contracts and has no human leadership or control. Imagine a fleet of self-driving cars whose onboard computers decided which passengers to pick up and when to drive to the gas station — these robots would be ruled by code, not humans. Or imagine a company where decisions were automatically made when a majority of employees voted for them (decisions would automatically go into effect thanks to a smart contract).[23] *Not to be confused with The DAO.*

DApp

Decentralized application (rhymes with "tap"); an app built with smart contracts. DApps' code is open-source and lives entirely on the blockchain. Compared to conventional centralized apps like Airbnb, Facebook, and Uber, DApps are more resilient (they don't fail if the company that made it goes out of business) and more transparent (decisions are made entirely by machines, not humans).[24]

Decentralization

When a network is not controlled by a single entity. If shopping at Walmart is centralized, shopping at a farmer's market is decentralized: goods flow straight from farmers to consumers, instead of going through Walmart. Cryptocurrencies are decentralized because (ideally) many people around the world track past payments and verify new payments; no one entity can control everything.

Deflation

When the growth of the money supply is less than the growth of the total value of goods and services produced (GDP, in economics terms). In other words, it's when inflation becomes negative and price levels go down. Deflation makes every dollar or coin worth more; this encourages people to hoard money instead of spending or investing it, which tends to reduce economic growth.[25]

Digital signature

A method used to verify the authenticity of digital messages such as blockchain transactions.[26] When you make a blockchain transaction (like sending someone cryptocoins), you use your private key to encrypt a small tag attached to the end of the transaction; anyone can then check the tag to make sure you were actually the one who sent it. *Also known as signature.*

Distributed ledger

A data structure that logs past transactions and isn't controlled by any one entity. Anyone can store a copy of the ledger and add their own entries if others approve. Blockchains are the best-known distributed ledger. *Also known as a decentralized ledger or shared ledger.*

DLT

Decentralized Ledger Technology. The umbrella term for any technology that stores data in a shared, distributed, immutable ledger; this includes blockchain and blockchain-inspired alternatives like the tangle.[27]

Double-spending

The risk that money will be spent twice; the biggest flaw of digital currencies. For instance, Word documents would make poor currencies because anyone can make infinite copies. Blockchains prevent this problem by tracking every time money changes hands, making it easy to notice when someone tried double-spending. Cryptocurrencies thus avoid this problem (unless they're hit with a 51% attack).[28]

ERC-20

The most popular type of Ethereum tokens. ERC-20 tokens follow a well-known set of rules, making them more predictable for users and easier to build for developers.[29] Many cryptocurrencies, including Maker (MKR) and the Basic Attention Token (BAT), are actually implemented as ERC-20 tokens, meaning that they actually run atop the Ethereum blockchain.[30]

Escrow

A place where money is temporarily held when two parties are transacting. The sender puts money in escrow, and it's only released when the receiver has fulfilled certain requirements. For instance, if you order something online, your money might get sent to escrow until the item is actually shipped to you, at which point the money will be released to the seller. Smart contracts and DApps often rely on escrow accounts.[31]

ETF

An exchange-traded fund, a financial asset that tracks the price of one or more stocks, cryptocurrencies, or other financial assets. An S&P 500 ETF, for instance, always sells at the value of the S&P 500 Index, which averages the prices of top stocks and is thus less volatile than buying individual stocks.[32] Cryptocurrency ETFs reduce volatility and also remove the hassle of setting up wallets, making them promising ways for average people to invest in crypto.[33]

Ether

The unit of currency used on the Ethereum network. Abbreviated as ETH.

EVM

The Ethereum Virtual Machine. Runs the code behind smart contracts. Each miner runs a copy of the EVM on their computers, since they need to execute smart contracts to mine blocks.[34]

Exchange

A website that lets you exchange fiat currencies such as the US dollar and yen for cryptocurrencies such as Bitcoin. You can often exchange cryptocurrencies for cryptocurrencies as well. *Also known as cryptocurrency exchange.*

Fiat

Currencies backed by faith in a government, such as US dollars, Japanese yen, and Indian rupees. Often contrasted with cryptocurrencies.

Fork

As a verb, refers to making a new branch to a blockchain. As a noun, refers to one of these new branches.[35] To take an analogy, imagine two co-authors wrote the first three novels in a five-part series but then split up and wrote their own versions of the fourth and fifth novels. Each author's version of the series would be a separate fork.

Full node

A node that downloads the entire blockchain. Cryptocurrencies need full nodes to stay decentralized — a cryptocurrency with just one full node is centralized around that one node and hence isn't any better than a regular currency. In Bitcoin, people who run full nodes aren't paid anything, so there are only a few thousand nodes (which many believe aren't enough). Solo miners have to run full nodes, but in a mining pool, only one person in the pool has to have a full node.[36]

Gas

A measure of the computing effort needed to run an Ethereum smart contract. Bigger, more complex smart contracts require more gas. When you use a smart contract, you pay miners a small fee for each unit of gas the smart contract consumed.[37] *See also Szabo and DApp.*

Genesis block

The first block in a blockchain and hence the oldest. Bitcoin's genesis block contains cryptic messages left by Satoshi Nakamoto, the inventor of Bitcoin.[38]

GPU

The Graphics Processing Unit, a special computer chip normally used to draw images on the screen. Computer graphics require a lot of math, so the GPU is good at running many complex math operations simultaneously. Cryptocurrency mining also happens to require a lot of complex math operations, so GPUs are quite good at mining — better than CPUs but still weaker than ASICs.[39]

Halving

When a cryptocurrency's block reward is cut in half, usually once every few years. Because of halving, block rewards slow down and eventually stop, causing the supply of cryptocoins to plateau.[40]

Hard fork

A radical, backward-incompatible change to a cryptocurrency that creates a brand-new cryptocurrency. Nodes that run the old software won't accept blocks accepted by the new software, so the blockchain permanently splits in two: one chain used by old-software nodes and one chain used by new-software nodes. The blockchain used by the new-software nodes effectively becomes the basis for a new cryptocurrency. Bitcoin Cash famously hard forked Bitcoin to allow bigger blocks.[41] *See also soft fork.*

Hardware wallet

A device that stores private keys and lets you authorize cryptocurrency transactions without ever putting your private key on your computer. This way, a hacker can't get your private key even if they can see everything on your computer. A form of cold storage.[42] *See also paper wallet.*

Hash

A (hopefully unique) fingerprint of a piece of data. Hashes are concise ways to refer to digital objects. In a store, a barcode number is a sort of hash for an item; writing down the barcode is much easier than writing down the entire product name and description, and it's easier to look up online as well. Hashes are core parts of cryptocurrencies, and mining usually requires you to compute trillions of hashes.[43]

Hashcash

The proof-of-work mining algorithm that Bitcoin uses. Miners' computers run the Hashcash algorithm billions and trillions of times, creating hashes that they hope will let them mine a block.[44]

Hash function

An algorithm that computes a hash, or fingerprint, for a piece of data; it's usually easy to compute the hash given the original data but hard to compute the original data given the hash.[45] A simple hash function for names might be to take their initials: it's easy to compute someone's initials given their name, but hard to figure out their name given their initials. (Does AE stand for Albert Einstein, Amelia Earhart, or someone else?) More sophisticated hash functions reduce the chance of "collisions," where two pieces of data yield the same hash value; ideally, hash values are all unique. *See also SHA-256.*

Hash rate

The speed at which a miner can generate hashes. Each hash gives miners a small chance of being chosen to mine the next block, so miners with higher hash rates have higher chances of mining a block and hence higher profits. The Bitcoin network's hash rate is the total hash rate of all Bitcoin miners put together.[46] *Also known as hash power.*

HODL

A slang term for irrationally holding onto cryptocoins no matter how bad the market gets, hoping for the next price spike. The term was born when someone drunkenly misspelled "hold" on a Bitcoin forum, but some people now humorously say it's an acronym for "hold on for dear life."[47]

Hot storage

Storing your cryptocurrency private keys on an internet-connected device, like your phone or laptop. This makes it more convenient to send money than cold storage — you can let your device autofill your private key instead of typing it in yourself — but also riskier, since a hacker with control over your device could easily grab your keys.[48] *See also cold storage.*

Howey test

A test the SEC uses to determine if an asset is a security. It says an asset is a security if "a person invests his money in a common enterprise and is led to expect profits solely from the efforts of the promoter or a third party."[49] Often invoked in debates over whether cryptocurrencies should be considered securities.

ICO

An initial coin offering. When a cryptocurrency or blockchain startup starts selling cryptocoins to raise money. A decentralized, unregulated alternative to IPOs; after a legal crackdown by the US, many crypto startups started offering STOs instead.[50]

Immutability

The inability to change. One benefit of blockchains is that they're practically immutable: barring a 51% attack, it's impossible to alter or remove a past transaction.

Inflation

When the growth of the money supply is greater than the growth of the value of goods and services (GDP, in economic terms). Inflation leads to increases in price levels and decreases in the value of currency; each coin or dollar can't buy as much "stuff" as it used to.[51] Some people say that inflation happens whenever the money supply grows (i.e. when more coins or dollars are created), but this isn't technically true — inflation is only when the money supply grows faster than economic output.

IoT

The Internet of Things; internet-connected sensors and devices like smart thermostats.

IPFS

The InterPlanetary File System. A protocol for decentralized file and webpage sharing over the blockchain. Designed to replace the centralized HTTP protocol for fetching webpages from websites, which has been called "slow, fragile, and forgetful" because information is lost if the central server goes down.[52]

IPO

When a non-crypto company starts listing stocks on public stock exchanges to raise money.

KYC

Know-Your-Customer regulations. Most crypto exchanges have to follow KYC regulations to prevent criminals from using their services for money laundering. Exchanges following KYC have to collect identification documents like photo IDs and credit card information from users. This reduces cryptocurrencies' anonymity (and thus one big reason to use them) but also makes life harder for criminals.[53] *See also AML.*

Ledger

A data structure that logs past transactions. Blockchains are ledgers, but so are Excel sheets that record a coffee shop's sales.

Lightning network

A proposed way to make Bitcoin scale better by doing some transactions off the blockchain. Two people who frequently send each other money would set up a wallet and each deposit some money in it; they could "pay" each other by just changing their balances in the wallet, without touching the blockchain. They could eventually shut down the wallet and get paid their balances. Only the setup and shutdown of the wallet would go on the blockchain.[54] Think of it like Splitwise for Bitcoin: writing down all the payments and only actually sending money when the dust has settled.

Lightweight node

A node that doesn't download the entire blockchain, which is many gigabytes in size. Instead, it uses SPV to ask a full node to check if transactions are valid. If you download a wallet app on your phone or use a web-based wallet, you're probably using a lightweight node. *See also full node.*[55]

Liquidity

A measure of how easy it is to turn an asset into cash. Stocks and cryptocoins are liquid because they can be sold in seconds, but a house is illiquid because it can take months or years to sell.[56]

Mainnet

The official, public blockchain where real monetary transactions happen. Compare to a testnet, which is a blockchain that developers use solely for testing.[57]

Market cap

The total value of all cryptocurrencies (or stocks) in circulation. This is just the number of coins times the value of each coin. A cryptocurrency's market cap is a common measure of how valuable and important the cryptocurrency is, just as a company's market cap is a measure of how powerful the company is.

Merkle tree

The data structure that the Bitcoin blockchain uses to store transaction data. The hash of each transaction depends on the hashes of all previous transactions, so a block's hash changes if any previous transaction was tampered with — making it easy to identify tampering.[58]

Micropayments

Small payments that usually happen online, such as buying an app for 99¢ or paying someone $2 to answer a survey. There's no rigid definition; some people say small offline transactions, like buying a $3 cup of coffee, are also microtransactions.[59] Microtransaction fees need to be low since they already make up a large percentage of the transaction's actual value. Cryptocurrencies, with relatively high fixed fees (over $1 for some currencies) are thus poorly-suited for microtransactions.

Middleman

An entity that stands between two people trying to communicate or transact. Facebook is the middleman if you're writing to a friend on Facebook Messenger; your bank is the middleman if you're wiring money; Amazon is the middleman if you're buying something off Amazon.com; and so on. Cryptocurrency and blockchains aim to get rid of middlemen.

MimbleWimble

A privacy-focused blockchain framework that's faster than Bitcoin's current blockchain framework, takes up 10 times less space, and hides the sender's and receiver's identities, as well as the amount sent. MimbleWimble backers want Bitcoin to replace its current blockchain software with blockchain software built on MimbleWimble; Grin and Beam are well-known examples of such software.[60]

Mining

When a cryptocurrency user validates transactions and competes for the privilege of adding a block to the blockchain. Mining is essential to stop double spending and increase the money supply, since miners' block rewards are the primary way for new coins to enter the economy.[61]

Mining pool

A group of cryptocurrency miners who share resources and profits. Mining pools are useful because setting up the infrastructure and equipment to mine is expensive and labor-intensive; it thus makes more sense to collaborate to set up a mining operation than to go it alone.[62] Bitcoin's mining pools are very powerful, collectively mining the vast majority of bitcoins — it's not profitable to mine solo anymore.[63]

Monetary policy

A central bank's ability to change the money supply by adjusting interest rates, buying and selling government securities, or other mechanisms.[64]

Money demand

The amount of wealth that people want to hold as cash, stocks, or other liquid assets for rapid spending. Money demand goes up when people want to make more purchases, such as during the holiday season.[65]

Money laundering

Passing illegally-obtained money through the financial system so it looks legal. For instance, a criminal could make fiat money selling stolen credit cards, anonymously turn that money into cryptocoins, and sell those coins for "clean" money.

Money supply

The total amount of currency and other highly-liquid assets in circulation. In the crypto world, this means the total number of cryptocoins in circulation.[66]

Multi-signature (multisig)

When multiple people's approval is needed for a cryptocurrency transaction to be made. For instance, a three-person company could set up a multisig scheme where at least two of the three people would need to approve any expenditures.[67]

Node

A phone or computer that runs the Bitcoin software. To buy or sell Bitcoin, you need to run a node. There are two major types of nodes: full (which store the entire blockchain) and lightweight (which don't).[68]

NFT

A non-fungible token: a token that represents a unique item, such as ownership over a particular song or video game item. NFTs aren't interchangeable (or "fungible"), while normal tokens and cryptocoins are: one bitcoin is the exact same as any other bitcoin, but a token representing a digital sword is very different than a token representing a digital dragon. NFTs are popular with crypto games like the cat-breeding game CryptoKitties or trading card games.[69]

Oracle

A services that let smart contracts get data from the outside world, such as the weather or stock prices. If you're making a DApp for sports betting, you'll need to use an oracle to get the latest sports scores and decide who to pay.

Paper wallet

A piece of paper that contains public and private keys to a cryptocurrency wallet, or "account." A popular method of cold storage, since it's impossible for online hackers to get this information. *See also hardware wallet.*

Peer-to-peer (P2P)

When two people can communicate and transact directly without having to go through a central entity. Making a credit card payment is not peer-to-peer, since money flows through large banks and credit card networks, but cash payments and cryptocurrency payments are peer-to-peer, since there's no single powerful entity in the middle. *See also client-server model.*

Peg

When the exchange rate between two currencies is fixed. A small currency usually "pegs" itself to a larger currency by offering a constant exchange rate. For instance, the Tether coin (USDT) is pegged to the US dollar: one USDT is always worth $1.[70]

Permissioning

Setting specific rules around who can access which data. Permissioned blockchains are popular with enterprises that make blockchain apps used by multiple people and companies, since it lets certain users (like CEOs) get full read/write access while restricting other users (like contractors) to a very specific set of data. Most blockchains let anyone view the whole history of transactions, but permissioned blockchains are the exception.[71]

Privacy coin

A cryptocoin that places a special emphasis on maintaining users' privacy and anonymity. Monero and ZCash are well-known examples.[72]

Private key

A secret code that lets you control the funds stored in a cryptocurrency wallet, or "account." The publicly-available public key and address can be computed from the private key, but it's almost impossible to compute the private key if you only have the public key or address. This is like the password on conventional apps.

Proof-of-stake (PoS)

A new mining scheme where miners put up their money as collateral; miners with more money at stake are more likely to be chosen to mine the next block. Miners who try to break the rules lose their deposits. Proof-of-stake is considered more energy-efficient than the competing proof-of-work scheme, since there's no arms race to run the most computations.[73]

Proof-of-work (PoW)

A mining scheme where miners that put in the most work (i.e. make the most hashes) are more likely to win. This makes tampering with the blockchain prohibitively difficult and expensive, since hackers would have to put in more work than everyone else. But it also leads to a lot of wasteful computation.[74] *See also proof-of-stake.*

Public key

A pseudonym for a cryptocurrency wallet, or "account," that anyone can see. Not used very often; people tend to use addresses instead to refer to cryptocurrency wallets. Addresses can be easily computed given the public key. *See also private key and address.*

Reserve currency

A currency used for major international transactions; commonly held by governments and central banks. Any currency can be a reserve currency, but the most common ones are the US dollar, the euro, the British pound, the Japanese yen, and the Chinese yuan.[75]

Ring signature

A privacy technique used in Monero. Multiple people are listed as potential senders for each transaction, so nobody can tell who really sent the money. One of Monero's major methods of maintaining privacy and anonymity. *See also stealth address.*

Satoshi

The smallest unit of Bitcoin, worth one hundred millionth of a bitcoin. Named in honor of Satoshi Nakamoto, the mysterious creator of Bitcoin.[76]

SEC

The US Securities and Exchange Commission. Regulates securities, investments, stock markets, and — now — cryptocurrencies.[77]

Security

An asset that you invest in, expecting to make a profit by betting on someone else's success. In 2017, the SEC announced tokens given out during ICOs were now considered securities and would be regulated as such.[78] *See also Howey test.*

SegWit

Segregated Witness (SegWit) was a soft fork of Bitcoin that increased the number of transactions allowed per block and thus the maximum number of transactions per second. The block size didn't change, but SegWit let transactions store some non-essential data outside the block, so transactions became smaller and more could fit in a block. Led to the hard fork of Bitcoin to make Bitcoin Cash because some people said SegWit didn't go far enough to improve transaction speed.[79]

Server

A powerful computer that powers websites and apps. Centralized apps have servers that all "clients," or user devices, talk to. If those servers go down, the app is unusable.

SHA-256

A one-way hash function that can compute the hash, or unique fingerprint, of any piece of data; it's easy to compute the hash given the data, but very hard to figure out the original data given just the hash. SHA-256 is used in Bitcoin's proof-of-work mining algorithm and Bitcoin's address-creation algorithm.[80]

Sidechain

A small blockchain that's tied to a bigger blockchain (or "main chain"); the main chain's currency can be used on the side chain. The sidechain can add extra features to the original cryptocurrency without launching a brand-new currency. For instance, the Liquid project seeks to increase the speed and privacy of Bitcoin. Instead of launching a wholly new token, it launched the Liquid Bitcoin (LBTC) token, which always trades at 1 BTC. Anyone can temporarily swap their BTC for LBTC, do some trades on Liquid, and turn their LBTC back to BTC.[81]

Single point of failure

A part of a system that, if it fails, takes down the whole system; the "weakest link."[82] Often refers to the middleman of centralized systems. If Facebook's servers go down, nobody can send Facebook messages, so Facebook is considered a single point of failure. In the real world, if there's only one rickety bridge crossing a river between two cities, that bridge is the single point of failure — if it breaks, nobody can travel between cities. Decentralization removes single points of failure, making systems more robust.

Silk Road

An infamous online drug market that used Bitcoin for payment. This was the first time many people had heard of Bitcoin, giving the currency reputation for enabling crime and lawlessness.[83]

Smart contract

A piece of code that lives on the blockchain and can move cryptocoins and tokens around based on certain rules. For instance, a poker smart contract could take in some coins from each player, compare everyone's hands at the end of the round, and automatically pay out the winner. Governed by code, not the legal system, as normal contracts are. Most commonly used in Ethereum. *See also DApps.*[84]

Soft fork

A backward-compatible upgrade to a blockchain. The blockchain temporarily splits into two branches (one used by nodes running old software, one used by nodes running new software), but once miners controlling the majority of hash power are on the new software, the branches merge and there's a single blockchain once again. Soft forks are how cryptocurrencies improve over time; cryptocurrencies have frequent soft forks without much fanfare.[85]

SPV

Simplified Payment Verification. A way for a lightweight node to make sure your and others' transactions are valid without having to download the entire blockchain. Instead, SPV asks full nodes, which have the full blockchain, to make sure all transactions are valid. Slightly less secure than having a full node, but good enough for most users.[86]

Stablecoin

A cryptocurrency that has a relatively stable exchange rate with major fiat currencies like the US Dollar. Tether (USDT) is a well-known stablecoin; it always trades at around $1.

Stealth address

A one-time address. Monero recipients get a new stealth address for every transaction. This hides recipients' real addresses and transaction history from the world. One of Monero's major methods of maintaining privacy and anonymity.[87] *See also ring signature.*

STO

Security Token Offering. A more regulated version of an ICO created to comply with new laws. To make fraudulent fundraising (a big problem with ICOs) harder, regulations often restrict how much money STOs can raise and who can invest in them.[88]

Szabo

A small unit of Ethereum, worth one-millionth of an ether (ETH). Named in honor of the legendary cryptocurrency and blockchain researcher Nick Szabo.[89] Ethereum gas prices are often quoted in szabos.[90]

Tangle

A blockchain competitor that stores transactions not in a list but in a spaghetti-like data structure. New transactions have to verify two randomly-chosen unverified transactions.

There's no mining (and hence no waits and lower fees), and many new transactions can be added in parallel.[91] For these reasons, the tangle is seen as ideal for the Internet of Things (IoT), which features many small devices logging data at the same time.[92] Created by the startup IOTA.

Testnet

A testing environment where developers can simulate a blockchain and thus test out new blockchain apps. None of the cryptocoins or tokens made on testnets are worth real money.[93] *See also mainnet.*

The DAO

A famous attempt to create a DAO, The DAO was an Ethereum project that was a sort of crowdsourced, automated venture capital firm. People would invest money in The DAO and vote on projects to fund — and smart contracts would ensure that the DAO automatically invested in whatever got the most votes.[94] But in 2016, The DAO was hacked and $50 million in ether was stolen; there was no way to undo the hack besides hard forking Ethereum (which Ethereum leaders did).[95] This highlights the problem with DAOs: when code is law, bugs and hacks can't be fixed or worked around.

Token

A virtual item, tracked on a blockchain, that represents the ownership of some asset. You could represent land, stocks, oil barrels, or any other asset with tokens.[96] Ethereum is the most popular blockchain platform for tokens. Tokens are remarkably flexible: some cryptocurrencies are actually implemented as Ethereum tokens![97] *See also ERC-20.*

Tokenization

Creating a token to represent some real-world asset. "Tokenizing land ownership" or "putting land on the blockchain" just means creating tokens that represent ownership of plots of land. Most of these tokens live on the Ethereum blockchain.[98] *See also ERC-20.*

TPS

Transactions per second; a measure of how much volume a payment network can handle. Many cryptocurrencies are criticized for their low TPS, which means the network gets congested when many people are trying to send money; congestion leads to high transaction fees and long waiting times.[99]

Transaction fee

A small amount that people sending cryptocurrencies pay to miners. Every transaction can specify a fee it's willing to pay; miners choose which transactions to include in the next block, so transactions that offer higher fees are typically picked first and thus added to the blockchain faster. These fees are one of the two sources of income for miners, the other being block rewards.[100]

Turing-complete

A programming language or platform that can do any possible computation, given enough time and hard drive space. Most smart contract platforms, such as Ethereum, are Turing-complete; that is, you can do any kind of computation in a smart contract.[101] This is often contrasted with Bitcoin's simple scripting language, which isn't Turing-complete and hence isn't powerful enough to run all kinds of computation.[102]

Txn

A common abbreviation for "transaction."

UTXO

Unspent transaction output. Cryptocurrency is a bit like cash in that there are "bills" and "change." If your real-world wallet has $23, you won't have a $23 note — you'll probably have four $5s and three $1s. When you go to buy a $4 coffee, you hand the cashier a $5 bill and get a $1 bill back. Cryptocurrency transactions work similarly: your account balance is made of several chunks of change, known as UTXOs. When you send someone money, you combine your UTXOs and send them part of it; the "change" returns to your account as a new UTXO.[103]

Vanity address

A cryptocurrency address that has a special series of characters. They're no better or worse than regular addresses, but they just look cool; they're similar to custom license plates on a car. For instance, the Internet Archive's Bitcoin address is *1Archive1n2C579dMsAu3iC6tWzuQJz8dN*.[104] Anyone can create an unlimited number of addresses, each with random characters; you just have to keep rolling the dice until you happen to get one that has the desired character sequence.[105]

Volatility

How much the price of an asset fluctuates. Cryptocurrencies, especially Bitcoin, are known for their high volatility, which makes them risky investment assets and inefficient currencies for everyday transactions.[106]

Wallet

A tool used to manage your cryptocurrency holdings. Some wallets are apps that let you send and receive money. Other wallets are physical objects — like USB sticks or pieces of paper — that just hold the private keys to a cryptocurrency "account." Also used to refer to your cryptocurrency "account" itself.

Whitepaper

A document published by people launching a new blockchain project or cryptocurrency. Whitepapers describe the project's motivations, how it works, and why it's valuable. They're designed to persuade people to invest in the project's ICO, and as such you should think of whitepapers more as advertisements than rigorous research papers.[107]

Zero-knowledge proof (ZKP)

A method that to prove you know something without revealing what it is. If someone wants to know that a laptop is yours, you don't have to tell them your password — you can just log into the laptop to prove that you own it, without revealing any password or account information. Zcash and Monero use this concept to obscure the details of transactions, such as the sender's and receiver's identities and the amount sent.[108]

Cryptocurrencies

The cryptocurrency space is massive and hard to follow: there are thousands of coins out there, each with their own special features and goals. Here, we'll give brief descriptions of some of the top cryptocurrencies by market cap, or the total value of all coins in circulation.

The ticker symbol for each cryptocurrency is listed first, then its name. In the crypto world, ticker symbols are often used as shorthand names for the coins they represent, and you'll also see them on graphs and financial websites.

BAT: Basic Attention Token

An Ethereum-based token used in the privacy-focused browser Brave. BAT aims to make online advertising fairer by sending more ad revenue to websites and protecting internet users' privacy. Advertisers pay internet users and publishers (sites that show the ads, such as the *New York Times*) each time users view an ad.[109] You can also tip your favorite Twitter users with BAT.[110]

BCH: Bitcoin Cash

A well-known hard fork of Bitcoin that increased the block size. This lets the network process transactions faster, thus reducing fees and waiting time.

BNB: Binance Coin

A cryptocurrency promoted by the popular cryptocurrency exchange Binance. Binance promotes the coin by giving a discount on transaction fees if you pay with BNB, so BNB investors are betting that Binance will grow in popularity. Binance's Launchpad product lets you buy tokens from ICOs; BNB is the only accepted form of payment.[111]

BSV: Bitcoin SV

A fork of Bitcoin Cash, which was itself a fork of Bitcoin. Craig Wright, the eccentric creator of Bitcoin SV, believed that Bitcoin Cash is too radical a departure from Satoshi's original vision for Bitcoin, so he made this fork that behaves much more like the technology laid out in the original Bitcoin whitepaper. [112]

BTC: Bitcoin

Bitcoin is the original, most famous, biggest, and most important cryptocurrency. It was invented by Satoshi Nakamoto in 2008; Bitcoin fans speculate that Satoshi was fed up with the banking system after the financial crisis hit.

BTG: Bitcoin Gold

A Bitcoin fork that uses an ASIC-resistant proof-of-work mining algorithm, which means that specialized mining rigs no longer have a massive edge in the mining game.[113] Thus, Bitcoin Gold claims to make mining more democratic. It's also noted for suffering a crippling 51% attack in 2018,[114] where attackers double-spend $18 million worth of coins. [115]

DASH: Dash

A cryptocurrency focused on everyday micropayments, such as buying coffee at a local shop. Dash aims to be more beginner-friendly than Bitcoin and offer lower fees and faster transactions than Bitcoin.[116] (Recall that Bitcoin has relatively high fees and slow transactions, making it ill-suited for micropayments.)

DOGE: Dogecoin

A rebranded clone of Litecoin, originally created as a joke based on the popular "Doge" meme,[117] which features a confused-looking Shiba Inu dog surrounded by silly phrases like "much donation" and "very coin."[118] Dogecoiners famously raised $25,000 to send the Jamaican bobsled team to the 2014 Winter Olympics.[119]

EOS

An Ethereum competitor that claims to offer faster transactions and lower fees.[120] Like Ethereum, you can build DApps and smart contracts on EOS.

ETC: Ethereum Classic

The older version of Ethereum. Ethereum Classic suffered a major hack in 2016, when $50 million was stolen from a decentralized venture capital organization known as the DAO. Most ETC users decided to make a hard fork of ETC that rolled back the theft; this new cryptocurrency became known as just Ethereum (ETH). ETC didn't roll back the theft and continued to exist as a separate currency, but ETH has grown far bigger than its older sibling, ETC.[121]

ETH: Ethereum

Perhaps the most famous and important cryptocurrency after Bitcoin, Ethereum offers smart contracts that let developers build decentralized apps (DApps) on the blockchain. Each time you use a smart contract, you pay a small fee for each action the smart contract takes. This fee is paid in ether (ETH), which can be bought and sold like a normal cryptocurrency.[122]

LINK: Chainlink

Chainlink is a specialized service, known as an "oracle," that lets smart contracts access data about the real world (weather, stock prices, etc.) in a decentralized way. If your DApp needs to get the current temperature, it can use Chainlink to get that data instead of relying on a centralized service like

AccuWeather. You pay for these information requests using the LINK coin.[123]

LTC: Litecoin

The original altcoin, Litecoin was designed to be the "silver to Bitcoin's gold." It offers faster transactions, lower transaction fees, and a less power-hungry mining algorithm than Bitcoin. The different mining algorithm is particularly interesting: Litecoin backers say it makes it harder for a few powerful miners to monopolize the mining space.[124]

MIOTA: IOTA

IOTA is a crypto startup focused on the internet of things (IoT). IOTA does away with the blockchain and instead lets you track transactions in the "tangle," a spaghetti-shaped data structure that offers faster and cheaper transactions than a blockchain.[125] You pay for IOTA with MIOTA coins.

MKR: Maker

Maker is a smart contract platform, like Ethereum, that lets you buy and sell stablecoins known as Dai; one Dai is pegged to $1. This is very useful for creating, say, a decentralized bank: people can lend and borrow money without having to worry about wild fluctuations in price. You pay for transactions on the Maker platform with the MKR coin.[126]

NEO

An Ethereum competitor backed by the Chinese government. (Meanwhile, Ethereum is run by a governing body made of many Western tech and finance companies.[127]) There are some technical differences between NEO and Ethereum, but they're similar enough that NEO is known as "the Ethereum of China."[128]

TRX: TRON

TRON is an ambitious crypto-startup that is building a decentralized content-sharing platform. In other words, it wants to cut out middlemen like Google Play and Netflix that stand between people who make digital media (movies, books, etc.) and consumers.[129] It's built atop IPFS, which you'll recall allows decentralized file sharing. TRX is an Ethereum-based token used to pay on TRON, and, interestingly, you can't mine TRX.[130]

USDT: Tether

The best-known stablecoin, the Tether coin (USDT) always trades at $1. Tether is built on the Ethereum blockchain and holds $1 for every USDT in existence to make sure it can always honor the conversion rate.[131] Tether also maintains coins pegged to 1 Euro, known as EURT.[132]

XEM: NEM

NEM lets you track any kind of asset — health records, loans, stocks, and so on — on a blockchain.[133] It's a business-focused product; a bank could use NEM to track loans and account balances on a private blockchain, or a government could store key documents like birth certificates on a private blockchain.[134] Besides its enterprise focus, NEM is known for its incredible versatility: it claims any app can integrate the NEM blockchain using any programming language.[135] The XEM coin is used to pay for transactions.[136]

XLM: Stellar

Stellar is a payments system that aims to make it easy, quick, and cheap to send money between countries. Under the hood, trusted entities called "anchors" in the sender's country convert the sender's money to cryptocoins called Stellar

Lumens (XLM), the Lumens are sent, and anchors in the recipient's currency convert the Lumens back to fiat.[137] Stellar is a fork of Ripple, and the two remain similar in terms of technology, but Ripple is a for-profit company that focuses on businesses and banks, while Stellar is a nonprofit that focuses on individuals and the unbanked.[138]

XMR: Monero

A privacy-focused cryptocurrency whose mining algorithm is ASIC-resistant, making it a good choice for independent, small-time miners.[139] Transactions are totally untraceable; the sender's and receiver's addresses aren't revealed, and nobody can even see how much was sent.[140] However, the anonymity and simplicity of mining makes Monero the favorite coin of cryptojackers, who install Monero mining scripts on hacked websites.[141]

XRP: Ripple

Ripple is an international payment network designed to help people move money around the world quickly and cheaply. Money transfer fees and delays are so high because today's payment systems don't interoperate well; Ripple provides a common tech layer that lets payment systems interact easily.[142] You can send any currency on Ripple — Euros, bitcoins, you name it — but Ripple is promoting its own cryptocurrency, known as XRP. Ripple isn't built on XRP, and Ripple users don't have to use XRP; XRP is just one of many possible currencies you can send with Ripple.[143]

XTZ: Tezos

A smart contract platform and competitor to Ethereum. It raised $230 million in its ICO, but the launch of the XTZ tokens was delayed for months due to battles between Tezos's founders and board of directors. These battles culminated in four class action lawsuits and heavy fines slapped on the founders.[144] It goes to show how cryptocurrencies aren't as decentralized as they may seem; ownership struggles still affect them.

ZEC: Zcash

Zcash is a privacy-focused cryptocurrency. Transactions are still logged on a public blockchain, but thanks to "zero-knowledge proofs," transactions can be verified without publicly revealing who sent the money, who received it, or how much was sent.[145]

Index

Notes

The world of blockchains and cryptocurrencies is so deep, and in *Bubble or Revolution* we've only scratched the surface. In this final section, we've provided links to every single source we used during our research.

To keep the paperback slim, we've put the links on our website at bubbleorrevolution.com/notes/2.2.0. If a particular fact or opinion piques your interest, we encourage you to read the source and dive deeper into the material!

Made in USA - North Chelmsford, MA
1246965_9780578528151
05.04.2021 0934